T0323589

Cambridge Elements ≡

Elements in Leadership
edited by
Ronald E. Riggio
Claremont McKenna College
Susan E. Murphy
University of Edinburgh
Founding Editor
Georgia Sorenson
University of Cambridge

NETWORK LEADERSHIP

Promoting a Healthier World through the Power of Networks

Jeffrey Beeson
Chief Enabling Officer
Ensemble Enabler

CAMBRIDGE
UNIVERSITY PRESS

Shaftesbury Road, Cambridge CB2 8EA, United Kingdom

One Liberty Plaza, 20th Floor, New York, NY 10006, USA

477 Williamstown Road, Port Melbourne, VIC 3207, Australia

314–321, 3rd Floor, Plot 3, Splendor Forum, Jasola District Centre, New Delhi – 110025, India

103 Penang Road, #05–06/07, Visioncrest Commercial, Singapore 238467

Cambridge University Press is part of Cambridge University Press & Assessment, a department of the University of Cambridge.

We share the University's mission to contribute to society through the pursuit of education, learning and research at the highest international levels of excellence.

www.cambridge.org
Information on this title: www.cambridge.org/9781009572026

DOI: 10.1017/9781009392242

First published 2024

A catalogue record for this publication is available from the British Library

ISBN 978-1-009-57202-6 Hardback
ISBN 978-1-009-39223-5 Paperback
ISSN 2631-7796 (online)
ISSN 2631-7788 (print)

Additional resources for this publication at www.cambridge.org/Beeson

Network Leadership

Promoting a Healthier World through the Power of Networks

Elements in Leadership

DOI: 10.1017/9781009392242
First published online: November 2024

Jeffrey Beeson
Chief Enabling Officer
Ensemble Enabler

Author for correspondence: Jeffrey Beeson, beeson@ensembleenabler.com

Abstract: A "paradigm shift" is currently taking place in leadership. Despite the considerable and influential body of existing theory, leaders were not prepared for the continuous disruptions of the digital era. What happens and how it happens depends on networks. The newly emerging science of networks opens an entirely new horizon on how to lead people, design organizations, and make sense of complex social environments. To be effective, leadership needs to assimilate and adapt to the dynamics of networks. This implies a focus on the quality of connections, how energy and information flow through these connections, and the development of a heightened awareness for the whole. Based on the undeniable logic of networks, the shift in organizational structures which has already taken place will only accelerate in the years to come. Network leadership invites leaders to leave the VUCA world behind and embrace a new WISE world of stability and emergence.

This Element also has a video abstract: www.cambridge.org/CELE-Beeson

Keywords: leadership mindset, interconnectedness, organizational structure, systems thinking, well-being

ISBNs: 9781009572026 (HB), 9781009392235 (PB), 9781009392242 (OC)
ISSNs: 2631-7796 (online), 2631-7788 (print)

Contents

1 The Power of Networks

A paradigm is a set of shared assumptions, beliefs, and methodologies that define a particular scientific discipline during a certain period. It provides a framework within which scientists conduct their research and interpret their findings.

Kuhn argued that scientific progress is not a linear and continuous process but is punctuated by "paradigm shifts" (Kuhn, 1962). These shifts represent times when the existing paradigm can no longer explain or accommodate new observations, anomalies, or challenges. As a result, a new paradigm emerges. This paradigm often displaces the previous one and leads to a radical transformation in the way science is conducted.

We are currently experiencing a "paradigm shift" in leadership.

A paradigm shift begins with anomalies; for instance, that data does not fit within the current paradigm's framework. This gives rise to a sense of crisis. Alternative frameworks emerge, which offer a new set of assumptions and perspectives. Only when one of these alternative frameworks gains dominance does a paradigm shift occur.

Something Seems to Be Missing

There is a large body of work in the field of leadership. This research aims to understand leadership from the various individual, team, organizational, and societal dimensions.

The examination of traits and behaviors of individual leaders has a long tradition at the **individual dimension**. Much effort has gone into devising instruments that determine personality traits and preferences. This perspective has been expanded by contingency theory (Fiedler, 1964), that is, how different behaviors are required in different situations.

Group development theory (Tuckman, 1965) introduced a **team dimension**. Belbin focused on identifying different roles that individuals naturally adopt within a team setting (Belbin, 1981). More recently Edmondson has highlighted psychological safety as a major factor in team learning (Edmondson, 2018).

With the publication of his book "Organizational Culture and Leadership" in 1989, Edgar Schein emphasized the **organizational dimension**, which tied leadership directly to organizational culture (Schein, 1989). Leading thinkers like Bennis, Collins, Covey, Drucker, Handy, Senge, and Sinek among others have emphasized the role of beliefs, values, purpose, and vision within organizations.[1]

---

[1] See Bennis (1989), Collins (2002), Covey (1990), Drucker (1974), Handy (1994), Senge (1990), and Sinek (2011).

At the level of the **social dimension** of leadership, Burns made a distinction between transactional and transformational leadership based on his observations of political leaders (Burns, 1978). Transformational leadership emphasizes a leader's ability to inspire and motivate followers toward achieving a collective vision. McCarthy developed his resource mobilization theory to explain how social movements mobilize resources and leadership attains their goals (McCarthy & Zald, 1977).

Despite this considerable body of theory, leaders have not been prepared for the continuous disruptions taking place since entering the digital era.

The first edition of the Encyclopedia Britannica appeared in 1768. Entries have always followed a rigorous review process. Articles are written by subject experts and edited by a central committee. The encyclopedia's editorial standards and emphasis on accuracy and reliability have made it a trustworthy source of information for centuries (Levy et al., 2023).

In 1998, Richard Stallman proposed the idea that no central organization should control the editing process. The founders of Nupedia – an encyclopedia organized along traditional centralized editorial processes – took up this idea. Wikipedia was launched on January 15, 2001.[2]

Wikipedia allows anyone with internet access to edit its articles. It is a dedicated community of editors who help maintain the site's quality and standards. Discussion spaces serve as a forum for collaboration and the revision of articles. The result? As of 2021, Wikipedia had entries of over ca. 61 million articles in contrast to Encyclopedia Britannica's ca. 120,000 entries.[3]

Wikipedia currently offers official versions in 334 languages. The Encyclopedia Britannica is primarily English based. Monthly visits to Wikipedia number about 15 billion page views per month while Britannica's website traffic is about 150 million per month (Gertner, 2023).

Welcome to the Power of Networks

And networks are everywhere.
The more we look, the more we find networks.

A **network** refers to an interconnected system or structure composed of nodes (individual entities) that are linked together by various connections, pathways, or relationships (see Figure 1).

---

[2] https://en.wikipedia.org/wiki/History_of_Wikipedia; "History of Wikipedia," accessed August 14, 2023.

[3] https://en.wikipedia.org/wiki/Encyclop%C3%A6dia_Britannica; "Encyclopedia Britannica," accessed August 16, 2023e.

Figure 1 A networked world. Image from www.vectorstock.com/royalty-free-vector/world-people-network-diagram-vector-20745425

These systems come in many forms such as computer networks, biological networks, neural networks, social networks, communication networks, transportation networks, energy networks, financial networks, and so on (Barabási & Pósfai, 2016, p.24).

Examples of networks are:

- The communication infrastructure that integrates billions of cell phones with computers and satellites.
- The electric grid that connects power plants, substations, and transformers with individual homes and businesses.
- Our brains – a network of billions of neurons.
- Viral infection spread – a network phenomenon.

Networks can be found everywhere. Recent research has shown that trees in a forest are connected to each other through their root systems and via fungal networks. Through these connections, trees are able to communicate and share resources with each other. This phenomenon has been dubbed the "*wood wide web*" (Simard, 2021, pp. 165–166).

Life Organizes Itself through Networks

Barabási, one of the pioneers in the science of networks, underscores the importance and omnipresence of networks in this way: "*Behind* **each** *complex system, there is an intricate network that encodes the interactions between the system's components*" (Barabási & Pósfai, 2016, pp. 23–24).

Complex systems refer to a collection of interconnected components that exhibit the following key characteristics (Chan, 2001):

- **Feedback loops**

  The output of a process influences the input of another process leading to a continuous cycle of adjustment, modification, and reinforcement

- **Nonlinear causality**

  The relationship between cause and effect is nonlinear, that is, small changes can lead to disproportionally large outcomes

- **Adaptation**

  Complex systems adapt, evolve, and self-organize in response to changes in their environment

- **Emergence**

  The properties of the whole system are not necessarily deducible from the properties of individual parts

- **Unpredictability**

  Due to nonlinear causality and emergence, the behavior of complex systems is often unpredictable

ALL living systems are complex systems. In other words, **life is based on networks**.

Despite the fundamental role that networks play, academic exploration linking leadership to networks has been sparse. However, the more that is learned about networks, the more this underscores their importance for leadership.

Duncan Watts describes how the perception of networks' truly dynamic nature is shifting:

> Networks have been viewed as objects of **pure structure** whose properties are **fixed in time** (emphasis from original). Neither of these assumptions could be further from the truth.
>
> First, real networks represent populations of individual components that are actually **doing something** – generating power, sending data, or even making decisions. Although the structure of the relationships between a network's components is interesting, it is **important** principally because it affects either their individual behavior or the behavior of the system as a whole.
>
> Second, networks are dynamic objects not just because things happen in networked systems, but because the networks themselves are evolving and changing in time, driven by the activities or decisions of those very components.

In the connected age, therefore, **what happens and how it happens depend on the network**. And the network in turn depends on what has happened previously. It is this view of a network—as an integral part of a continuously evolving and self-constituting system – that is truly new . . . . (Watts, 2002, pp. 27–28)

Structure of This Cambridge Leadership Elements Edition

In this edition of the Cambridge Elements Leadership series, I assert that both organizations and communities are complex systems based on networks. Leadership needs to adapt to the dynamics of networks to be effective.

In the sections that follow, the interrelationship between leadership and networks is explored from a variety of perspectives.

Section 2 looks at the emerging science of networks, highlighting the key principles that are of paramount importance for leadership.

Section 3 examines how the logic of networks impacts what effective leaders do. Two new metaphors emerge to describe leadership in an interconnected era.

Section 4 views the impact of networks on the structure of organizations. The logic of networks is changing how human beings collaborate.

Section 5 revisits the age-old question: What is the raîson-d'être of leadership? A network perspective provides a compellingly clear response.

2 Connection and Contagion

Relativity and quantum mechanics – the physics of the very large and the very small – were two of the major scientific developments in the twentieth century. These discoveries have had an immense impact on our understanding of the universe and on technological developments. However, these scientific endeavors addressed issues that are not part of an average person's everyday experience.

A Science of Our Everyday World

Network science is a new science that has come of age during the first two decades of the twenty-first century. It is **focused on the everyday world**. It explores how connections shape and influence us and the world around us. Network patterns form the backbone of complex systems such as life.

Issues that are important for leaders to understand and assimilate into their personal practice are highlighted in this section. In the sections that follow, the implications of network science for leadership and organizations in the twenty-first century are explored.

Network science was born in 1735 when Swiss mathematician Leonard Euler resolved the seven Bridges of Königsberg challenge (Carlson, 2023).

In this challenge, there are two islands located in a river that flows through the heart of the city. These islands are connected via seven bridges (see Figure 2).

The citizens of Königsberg (modern-day Kaliningrad) had developed an unusual pastime. Newcomers to the city were challenged to cross each bridge just once without re-crossing any one of them.

Euler proved that this was not possible (Euler, 1741).

As mathematicians are wont to do, Euler delved further into this challenge to generalize a solution that would be applicable for any number of landmasses and bridges.

> If there are more than two landmasses with an odd number of connections, then crossing each bridge just once is not possible (In the diagram below, the landmasses A, B, C and D all have an odd number of bridge connections). If only one connection is removed – the bridge between landmass A and D for example – then a solution is possible. However, the crossing must begin at one of the landmasses (B or C) which has an odd number of connections. (Carlson, 2023)

This example illustrates the fundamental characteristics of networks: Networks are composed of **nodes** (landmasses), **links** (bridges), and **flows** (newcomers to Königsberg who cross the bridges) (See Figure 2).

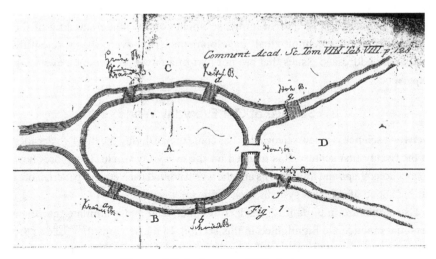

Figure 2 Euler's map of Königsberg.

These characteristics differ widely from one network to another. For example, in a logistics network, the **nodes** are different geographic locations; the **links** are the trucks, trains, and/or bicycles that travel between those locations; and the **flows** are the material goods that are transported from one location to another.

**The manner in which nodes are connected to each other
influences how flows travel throughout the network.**

Despite its early beginnings, only in the late 1990s did network science emerge as a rigorous data-driven science, fueled by the advent of computing power and the rise of the internet. Since then, network science has successfully been applied to a broad spectrum of applications ranging from preventing the spread of contagious diseases to combatting terrorism (Barabási & Pósfai, 2016, p. 24).

Given its data-driven character, it is understandable that leaders would consider network science as just another tool of data experts to help increase efficiency.

This understanding of network science would be fully missing the point. Network science opens a new horizon on how to lead people, design organizations, and make sense of complex social environments. While leaders do not need to understand the mathematics behind network science, it will become increasingly important for them to understand and internalize network science's fundamental concepts and principles.

Why? Because network science reveals how life and other complex systems such as organizations function.

What follows is an overview of some of these key concepts and insights.

It's a Small World After All

The small world principle asserts that any two nodes in a network are at most six connections (or degrees) separated from each other (Milgram, 1967). This principle is illustrated by the following scenario: a letter given to a rickshaw driver in New Delhi needs to go through only six pairs of hands before reaching the President of Peru (or for that matter any other person on the planet).

This phenomenon led to coining the phrase "six degrees of separation" (see Figure 3) and formed the basis for social trivia games such as the "Oracle of Bacon." [4]

The challenge in the "Oracle of Bacon" game is to determine how an actor or actress is connected to the actor Kevin Bacon. A computer program supports this game. It accesses a database that identifies the roles and movies

---

[4] https://oracleofbacon.org/

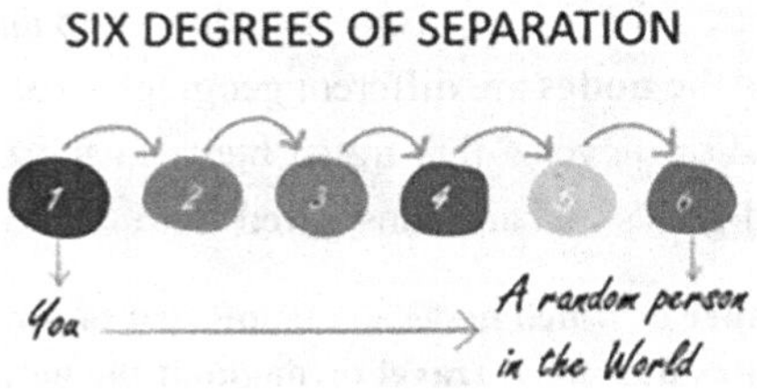

SIX DEGREES OF SEPARATION

Figure 3 Six degrees of separation. Image from https://neo4j.com/developer-blog/first-proof-of-six-degrees-of-separation/

of actors and actresses. Highlighting the actor Kevin Bacon is an historical accident. Almost any actor or actress could have been at the center of this game.

Here is an example of how the "Oracle of Bacon" game is played:

QUESTION: How is Marlon Brando connected to Kevin Bacon?

Brando starred in the film "A Dry White Season" with Donald Sutherland who starred in the film "JFK" with Kevin Bacon. In other words, Marlon Brando is only two degrees of separation away from Kevin Bacon.

The Power of Weak Links

How is such extreme connectivity possible? It boggles the mind to realize that any two people out of approximately 8.1 billion inhabitants on the planet are only "6 handshakes of separation" apart.

The most cited publication in network science "The strength of weak ties" (Granovetter, 1973) described what makes this possible. "*When it comes to acquiring important information such as finding a job or meeting a partner, our weak social ties are usually more important than our selected strong friendships*" (Granovetter, 1973, p. 1361). In other words, one is more likely to get a tip for a new job from someone whom one does not know very well, than from a family member.

People live in "clusters" that consist of small circles of people including family and friends. The average American has between two and six close or "strong" social ties. People in the same cluster typically have similar social ties. To access new social connections, one must **activate** the "weak" ties. These are people who belong to other clusters. New worlds open up when we reach out to other clusters.

"Weak ties" make the six degrees of separation possible. They allow individuals to reach people who are very distant to them in a network.

In the play "Six Degrees of Separation" (Guare, 1990), John Guare encapsulates this phenomenon in a truly memorable way:

It's a profound thought.
How every person is a new door, opening up into other worlds.

When You Smile, the World Smiles with You

Network science focuses on how data travels through networks. However, data is not the only – *and may not be the most important* – information that flows through a network of people.

Experiments demonstrate that people can "catch" emotional states they observe in others over time frames ranging from seconds to weeks (Scollon et al., 2003). The ability to sense what others are feeling is instinctive and has even been identified in toddlers (see Figure 4) who have not yet learned to speak (Gulick, 2023).

This is also instinctive in a team or organization. For example, if one member is enthusiastic about a project, their emotions can spread to other team members. This in turn boosts overall motivation. Conversely, if a member is consistently negative, it can impact the mood of the entire team.

Networks help to spread intangibles such as emotions, attitudes, values, beliefs, and behaviors as well as data and information. These diverse items can be clustered under the label of "energy." Emotions, values, beliefs, and behaviors can inspire and motivate others – in other words – produce "energy." On the other hand, certain attitudes or feelings can lead to fear and depression and, as a result, "de-energize." Seen from this perspective, energy is continuously increasing or decreasing because of our interactions.

Networks disseminate both information and energy.

Figure 4 Contagion. Image from https://imgflip.com/memetemplate/
173036543/Two-crying-babies

This transfer of "energy" can have a substantial impact. Studies have confirmed that people are more likely to be overweight if other people in their network are overweight. They are also more likely to go on a diet if other people in their network are dieting. An individual is more likely to vote if people in their network are voting. With respect to the pursuit of happiness, the choice of connections is vital. The happier people are in a personal network, the more likely that individual will be happy as well (Christakis & Fowler, 2009, Chapter 2).

In a research project undertaken in business organizations, participants were requested to identify individuals in the organization as "energizers" and "de-energizers." **Energizers** are those individuals who emanate "energy" through their interactions with others (i.e., inspire them, help them to engage more fully). **De-energizers**, on the other hand, have the opposite effect.

The research findings (Cross et al., 2003) showed that energizers are:

- more likely to have their ideas considered and put into action;
- get more from the people around them (i.e., people are more likely to devote discretionary time to an energizer's concerns);
- attract the commitment of other high performers;
- impact what individuals and networks learn over time, thus enhancing group learning.

In contrast, no matter how relevant the expertise of de-energizers is, it often goes untapped.

Three Degrees of Influence

The spread of influence in social networks obeys the "Three Degrees of Influence" Rule (Christakis & Fowler, 2009, pp. 28–30). Everything one does or says ripples through a personal network. This has impact on friends (one degree), friends' friends (two degrees), and even friends' friends' friends (three degrees). Personal influence gradually dissipates after that and ceases to have a noticeable effect on people who lie beyond the three degrees of separation.

The Three Degrees Rule of Influence implies that one can be indirectly influenced by people whom one has not met in person. Conversely, individuals have influence on people whom they may never meet.

Six degrees of separation refers to the structure of one's personal **connections**. The Three Degrees of Influence Rule applies to how people influence and can be influenced by their connections – or in other words – how "**contagious**" people are in their personal networks.

**Connection and Contagion are key properties which
influence the structure and function of social networks.**

Structure Is Destiny

Even though flows (i.e., information, resources, etc.) **can** travel from one node to another in a maximum number of six steps, doesn't mean that this occurs in most networks. The way flows are disseminated depends on the structure of the network itself. This is referred to as the network's **topography**. For example, the speed, extent, and patterns of spread of viral infections are greatly influenced by the structure of population networks (Alexander & Kobes, 2011).

> **The construction and structure of networks**
> **is the key to understanding the complex world around us.**
> **Albert-Laszló Barabási** (Barabási & Frangos, p.12)

Some of the key elements that determine network structures are:

Density and Centrality

DENSITY is the proportion of actual connections compared to the total connections possible (see Figure 5). **Low-density networks** represent systems where interactions are less common or limited. An example of a low-density industry is agriculture. Farms are typically spread out over large areas and each farm operates relatively independently.

High-density networks have more connections and exhibit quicker information distribution. A famous example of a high-density network is Silicon Valley, which is recognized as a nerve center for technology companies, startups, venture capitalists, and research institutes. The proximity and high connectivity of these groups fosters rapid innovation, idea sharing, and talent exchange.

CENTRALITY measures the relative importance and influence of individual nodes within a network. Various centrality measures capture different aspects of a node's importance (see Figure 6).

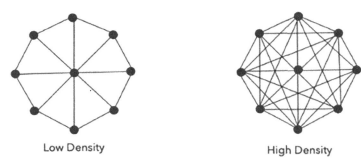

Low Density   High Density

Figure 5 Network density. Image from Watanabe (2021).

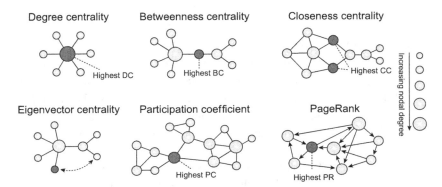

Figure 6 Measurements of centrality. Image from
Farahani et al. (2019).

- **Degree Centrality** measures the number of connections that a node has. The
  more connected nodes are the more influential they tend to be.

    Example: In a supply chain that consists of manufacturers, suppliers, and
    distributors, high-degree centrality could identify a node that is central to the
    overall supply chain.

- **Betweenness Centrality** measures the extent that a node lies on the shortest
  path between other nodes. Nodes with high Betweenness Centrality act as
  bridges between different parts of the network.

    Example: In disaster response networks, individuals or organizations that coord-
    inate and channel resources to affected areas characteristically exhibit a high level
    of Betweenness Centrality.

- **Closeness Centrality** measures how close a node is to all other nodes in
  terms of distance (i.e., degrees of separation). Nodes with high closeness
  centrality can quickly access other nodes in the network.

    Example: In academic collaboration networks, researchers with high closeness
    centrality can act as intermediaries for information exchange.

- **Eigenvector Centrality** measures the importance or influence of a node
  within a network. It is based on the idea that nodes are considered central if
  they are connected to other central nodes. It takes not only the number but the
  quality of connections into account.

    Examples: Opinion leaders on social and political issues are generally indi-
    viduals with a high Eigenvector Centrality.

- **PageRank Centrality** is inspired by the Google PageRank algorithm. This
  measurement is based on the idea that a node is important if it is linked to by
  other important nodes.

Example: In a start-up ecosystem, start-ups with strong ties to successful mentors or investors might be considered by venture capitalists to be more promising than others.

- The **participation coefficient** quantifies how well a node participates in different communities or clusters within a network. A node with a high participation coefficient has connections that span multiple clusters or communities.

Flow Inhibitors

Even though "weak ties" can be activated, many "weak ties" remain idle. A great potential can be awakened in most networks just by activating "weak ties."

Besides inertia, there is also a proactive component that suppresses flows. Gatekeepers are nodes within a network who control access to certain resources, information, opportunities, or relationships (Belardinelli, 2019). Gatekeepers shape the flow of information, control the diffusion of innovations, mediate relationships between different groups, and influence decision-making processes.

Gatekeepers often exhibit a high degree of centrality.

Directionality

In some networks, information flows in only one direction. In the internet, substantial portions of information only flow in one direction. One can click from page A to B to C to D, but a reverse path to get back to the starting point is not always an option.

This kind of directionality has consequences for the structure of a network. It limits its navigability and leads to the network's fragmentation into four so-called "continents." How each continent is connected to others differs. One continent is not accessible from the central core of the network (Barabási & Frangos, 2002, p. 169). Directionality is what makes the dark web of the internet possible. This is a portion of the internet that is not indexed by traditional search engines such as Google.

Clusters and Communities

Homophily is a very strong force in the structure of social networks (Christakis & Fowler, 2009, pp. 108–109). It is the tendency of individuals to associate and form connections with others who are similar to them, that is, in terms of age, gender, race, values, beliefs, social class, and so on.

Clusters refer to nodes that are more densely connected to each other than to nodes in other groups. Clusters reveal functional or thematic groupings.

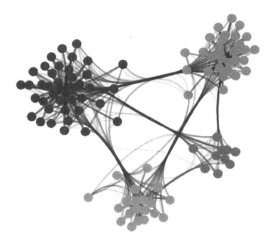

Figure 7 Detecting communities within networks. Image from
https://stackoverflow.com/questions/43541376/how-to-draw-communities-
with-networkx

For instance, network members working on the same project will tend to build clusters within networks.

The **cluster coefficient** measures the extent to which nodes in a network tend to cluster together. It quantifies the likelihood that "neighbors" of a node are also connected to each other (Watts & Strogatz, 1998).

Communities refer to subgroups within a network where individuals are more densely connected than with other nodes outside of that subgroup. By definition, all members of a community must be reachable through other members of the community (Barabási & Pósfai, 2016, p. 325). Communities often represent cohesive entities within a network such as a business' marketing department or a lean manufacturing team (see Figure 7).

Communities are defined by their structural connections, not necessarily by shared traits.

**Identifying clusters and communities helps to uncover hidden patterns,
understand functional relationships and reveal the dynamics of a network.**

The Rich Get Richer

Dreams of an egalitarian future formed during the initial heady years of the emerging internet. The internet would level social hierarchies and give everyone a voice. This techno-utopia would usher in a radical new age of equality. To the dismay of many, scientists have found that some of the key properties of networks do not support this vision.

Metcalfe's Law

This law was originally formulated for telecommunication networks.[5] It states that the value of a network is proportional to the square of the number of connected users of the system. In other words, the more users a network has, the more valuable it becomes to each individual user.

The last king of Hawaii, King Kalakaua liked to be at the forefront of technology. Soon after the Bell company was founded in 1877, Kalakaua had a phone installed in his palace. The legend goes that he had a phone even before one was installed in the White House. His phone was a mere curiosity at first. King Kalakaua had very few people whom he could actually call. The value of his phone only began to increase as more users came into the telephone system.[6]

The logic of Metcalfe's law is applicable in most networks. Most people use the term "network effect"[7] (Osman, 2023) to describe this positive feedback loop reaction.

This "network effect" is recognizable in everyday internet platforms. On YouTube as more creators upload content and more viewers watch and engage with videos, the platform becomes more valuable to both content creators and viewers.

In some cases, the network effect can lead to a "winner-take-all" scenario. Despite decades of billion-dollar investments in its Bing search engine, Microsoft has not been able to take much market share from Google.[8]

Preferential Attachment

Nodes that are highly connected are more likely to attract new connections. In a social network like LinkedIn, the probability that a new user will follow an existing member is not random. The choice of whom a new user will follow is influenced by the number of followers of the existing member. In other words, **the more followers a user has, the more likely they are to gain additional followers**. This results in a small number of nodes accumulating many connections over time.

---

[5] See www.techopedia.com/definition/29066/metcalfes-law

[6] www.ilind.net/2018/10/31/the-1885-honolulu-telephone-book/

[7] The term "network effects" was first used in the 1985 paper – Farrell, J.; Katz, M.; Saloner, G; "Network Effects, Competition, and Entry Barriers"; Journal of Economic Perspectives.

[8] As of March 2023, Microsoft had 8, 2 percent of the global desktop search market vs. 85, 5 percent for Google.

An example is the world of Hollywood actors. When a casting director chooses an actor or actress to play a part in a movie, they take various decision criteria into consideration. Two of the more important criteria are fit and popularity. Does this actor/actress fit the part? Are they popular? The more movies and actor or actress has featured in, the more likely they are to be popular. As Hollywood well knows, popularity sells movies. In addition, the more movies an actor or actress has made, the more likely that they will have been able to demonstrate their personal range of capabilities. This makes the qualification for a role more feasible. Aspiring new actors have a huge disadvantage. One needs to be known to get good roles. On the other hand, one needs to have good roles to be known. Most good roles are given therefore to actors or actresses who are already well established (Williams et al., 2019).

Scale-Free Networks

Until the late 1990s, network scientists believed that connectivity in complex networks was distributed randomly. This distribution is depicted by a typical Bell curve (see Figure 8).

This is not the property of real networks. Most nodes in real networks have only a few connections. Moreover, there are a few nodes that have an extensively large number of connections. This is due to the impact of preferential attachment.

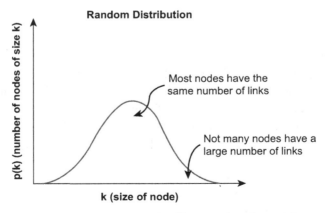

Figure 8 A random distribution of how nodes are connected. Image adapted from https://jitha.me/power-law-working-hard-enough/

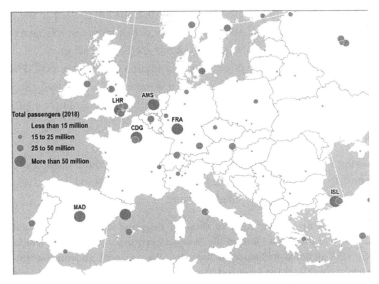

Figure 9 Airport network in Europe. Image from https://transportgeography
.org/contents/chapter6/airport-terminals/passenge-freight-airports-europe/

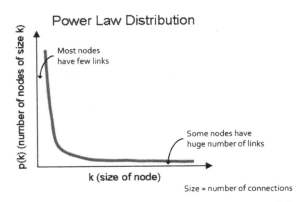

Figure 10 A power-law distribution of how nodes are connected. Image adapted
from https://jitha.me/power-law-working-hard-enough/

Complex networks function like air traffic networks (see Figure 9). There are
a lot of small airports that provide regional service and a few big hubs that
service the entire planet (Sun & Wandelt, 2021).

The connectivity distribution of these networks follows what is called
a power-law distribution (see Figure 10). This type of distribution is visible in

most networks. For example, power-law distributions are present in the distribution of income and wealth, the frequency of use of words in a language, the size of earthquakes, the distribution of internet traffic, and so on.

Networks characterized by power-law distributions have been named "scale-free." No matter how large a network gets, this pattern of connectivity stays the same.

The Invisible Hand

Discovering that most networks follow a power-law distribution was extremely significant. A leading network scientist, Albert László Barabási recounts the importance of identifying this characteristic:

> **Power laws are at the heart of some of the most stunning conceptual advances in the second half of the twentieth century ... Spotting them in networks signaled unsuspected links to other natural phenomena and placed networks at the forefront of our understanding of complex systems in general.** (Barabási & Frangos, 2009, p. 72)

Fritjof Capra contributes to this course of thought by stating: "There is a unified pattern of life, and we can be more precise and say that the pattern is a network pattern" (Pisani, 2007).

Self-Organization and Stability

Physicists and mathematicians have been very excited about finding power-law distributions in networks. Power-laws have been identified throughout nature in the transition from disorder to order. This transition is exemplified for instance in the phase transition of water into ice. **Order is maintained through the powerful forces of self-organization, which is made feasible by power-laws.** What is significant is that power-laws are not just another means to characterize a system's behavior. They are the distinct signature of self-organization in complex systems.

Self-organization refers to the process during which a system maintains a particular structure without external intervention. Self-organization is characterized by decentralized control and feedback loops. The interaction of many individual components in complex systems can be observed in the flocking behavior of birds or the flow of traffic.

Self-organization is observed every day in the economy. It is the "invisible hand" that Adam Smith posited in *The Wealth of Nations* (Smith, 1776, Chapter 2, p. 477).

Consider an open-air food market in the center of a large city. No central authority dictates what each agent should produce or sell. Farmers decide which crops to grow based on their understanding of the terroir and personal preferences. Vendors decide which products to offer based on their assessment of customer preferences and availability. Interactions are local – farmers negotiate with vendors, vendors bargain with customers, and customers provide feedback on product quality. Food markets exhibit order and organization despite the absence of centralized control. Over time, certain patterns emerge in response to customer preferences and market dynamics.

Self-organization works because larger hubs with a high degree centrality support the **stability** of the network. They create short paths between individual nodes that facilitate efficient information flow. In food markets, the larger producers and vendors tend to fill this role.

When surfing the internet, computer users experience this stability thanks to large hubs like Google's search engine that allows individual users on the web to connect through just a few clicks.

Resilience

Resilience refers to a network's ability to maintain its functionality even when confronted with disruptions or failures. A resilient network quickly recovers from such disturbances and continues to function without significant degradation.

Scale-free networks tend to be very resilient. If one of the many smaller nodes (those with few connections) fails, the information that travels through the network can be rerouted and the network's function can continue. For example: If a regional airport goes out-of-action in a specific airline travel network, the rest of the entire network will continue to function. In the meantime, solutions to resolve the affected region can be identified.

The emergence of the internet is a direct result of this resilience of networks. The initial aim of the internet was to ensure the resilience of the communication system in the case of a military attack.[9]

Redundancy is at the heart of resilience. It is essential to have multiple pathways, components, or resources that can perform the same function. This redundancy ensures that if one part of the network fails, there are alternative mechanisms that maintain connectivity.

The "Achilles' heel" of scale-free networks can be the high degree of centrality of large hubs themselves. If these hubs are **simultaneously** rendered inoperable, the entire network's functioning can be impacted. An example of this vulnerability was the regional power grid blackout of 2003.[10] This blackout resulted in a power outage in 265 power plants located in the Northeast and

---

[9] See "A Brief History of the Internet"; www.usg.edu/galileo/skills/unit07/internet07_02.phtml

[10] See www.history.com/this-day-in-history/blackout-hits-northeast-united-states

Midwest of the United States and in Ontario in Canada. An estimated 55 million people lost power. The proximate cause was a software bug in Ohio, which simultaneously impacted several hubs.

When Patterns Are Broken, New Worlds Emerge

Networks are not static. They change and shift as new nodes and links are added, or as existing nodes and links disappear. As networks evolve, certain critical points are reached when something truly amazing happens. The change in connectivity leads to new properties of the system arising, which were not previously present. This phenomenon is known as **emergence**.

When Connectivity Intensifies

The phase transition of water freezing into ice is a classic example of emergence. As temperatures decrease, water molecules start to form hydrogen bonds that allow them to come closer together. The formation of stable ice nuclei begins at a critical point. It is the ice nuclei that serve as the starting points for the growth of ice crystals. Water molecules increasingly join a crystal structure and, in the process, form a highly organized hexagonal lattice. Eventually, all the water is transformed from a liquid into a solid. It is the change in connectivity among the water molecules that allows this transition from water to ice to occur.

Changes in connectivity can change the properties of the whole.

A more mundane example is traffic congestion. A critical point emerges when the traffic flow suddenly transitions from free-flowing to congested. This congestion emerges from the interactions of many individual vehicles, not any single vehicle. Congestion becomes a collective behavior when the density of vehicles reaches a critical point. When reaching the critical point is imminent, both small changes in the number of vehicles or the behavior of one driver can have disproportionally large effects on the overall traffic flow.

A Few Extra Connections Can Make a Huge Difference

The original research into "six degrees of separation" discovered that just a few extra links are sufficient to drastically decrease the average separation between nodes (Watts & Strogatz, 1998). The separation between nodes amazingly collapses thanks to the long bridges that the new links form.

The researchers used a sport stadium as an illustration of this phenomenon.[11] Imagine a person who wants to get a message to someone at the other end of the

---
[11] See Talas (2021) Video 16:20 to 18:00.

stadium. If the only connection that they have is the person on either side of them, it will take a long time for the message to be transported across the entire stadium. Introduce just a few mobile phones into the equation. Suddenly the communication between different parts of the stadium becomes instantaneous. Only a few people with mobile phones can change the entire communication landscape within the stadium.

Adding a few extra nodes or links can have a startling outcome. As the COVID-19 pandemic began in 2020, the pharmaceutical company Pfizer possessed both the vaccine development and market distribution capability to make an impact. However, they had insufficient in-house knowledge of the breakthrough mRNA technology, which would allow a speedy introduction of a vaccine. Pfizer created a partnership with BioNtech, a small German biotechnology startup with a leading expertise in mRNA. Through this connection, Pfizer was able to become the market leader in COVID-19 vaccines. In contrast, Glaxo Smith Kline – the market leader in vaccines prior to the pandemic – did not find an appropriate mRNA partner. As a result, the company was unable to develop a vaccine and did not take advantage of one of the biggest historical market opportunities for vaccines (Kuchler & Abboud, 2021).

When Important Nodes Vanish

Removing links can have a similar effect. The properties of the whole network can change substantially when individual nodes disappear.

An example from the interaction between man and nature illustrates the impact of removing a key link. Kelp forests are an ecosystem located in cool, shallow waters close to the shore. In the early part of the twentieth century, kelp forests in California were receding and nobody knew why (Blackledge, 2023).[12] Every year the kelp forests became less healthy and produced a lower abundance of kelp.

Studies carried out by ecologists noticed that there was an overabundance of urchins in the ecosystem.

Urchins feed on kelp. The natural predator of the urchin is the sea otter. However, there was a scarcity of sea otters in the ecosystem because they had been hunted for their furs.

Sea otters are a keystone species that ensures the health of kelp ecosystems (Paine, 1969). By reducing the number of sea otters, the entire ecosystem system was threatened. Only when restrictions on the hunting of sea otters

---

[12] Apparently a recurrence of receding kelp forests is occurring again in northern California and Alaska – again due to a reduction in the otter population. This time the otters are being endangered by a change in climatic conditions.

were made and marketing campaigns dissuading consumers from buying sea otter furs were implemented, could the kelp forests recover.

Nonlinear Causality

Many of the changes that occur to a system as connections appear and/or disappear are **not predictable**. Because nodes are connected to multiple other nodes, changes in a system can create a web of interactions. These interactions lead to **feedback loops**, which either amplify or dampen initial causes. A small change can trigger a disproportionately large response or on the other hand, a large impulse may lead to no change at all.

Customer satisfaction processes in organizations illustrate this phenomenon. Improving customer satisfaction may not initially show any noticeable difference. However, a threshold can be reached. This occurs when customers are both satisfied and become loyal advocates of the brand. They start to refer the brand to others as well as continue to do business with the company. A substantial increase in customer loyalty and an influx of new customers is observed when this threshold is crossed (Reichfeld, 2011, Chapter 6).

The Whole Is Greater Than the Sum of Its Parts

The properties that emerge at the system level may not be detectable at the individual node level. When highly flammable hydrogen and oxygen combine, for example, they form water, which has completely different properties than its component parts.

Another example from nature further illustrates this point. Ants are relatively simple creatures when considered as individual insects. However, when they come together as a colony, complex behaviors such as foraging, nest building, and defense are exhibited. Ant colonies display a level of organization, division of labor, and problem-solving that is not apparent when ants are studied only individually (Kronauer, 2022).

Key Insights from Network Science Matter

Network science provides fundamental insights for leaders. It reveals how people connect and the way they influence each other through these connections. A broad spectrum of issues that demonstrate the power of networks have been presented in this section. These issues covered the impact of the degrees of separation and influence, the role of centrality, directionality, clustering, network effects, scale-free structures, self-organization, redundancy, unpredictability, emergence, and finally the properties of the whole being different than the properties of the parts.

The implication of these insights advocates for a reexamination of what comprises effective leadership. Just like the phenomenon of emergence in networks, a different image of effective leadership is beginning to emerge. This is the focus of the next section.

3 Acupuncturist or Gardner?

The key components of a network are its nodes, the connections between these nodes, and what flows through these connections.

Taking this into consideration, network science sends a simple message to leaders. Focus on the connections between people and what flows through these connections. Continue to focus on the attributes of the people (i.e., nodes) themselves and how they either accentuate or inhibit flows. In addition, endeavor to develop an acute awareness for the whole, which is ultimately greater than the sum of its parts.

This section will consider the implications for leaders when their focus shifts to the space between people. This is the space of connection and contagion.

Strengthen Flows

There is an inherent logic in exploring connections first and flows second. The network structure stemming from existing connections exerts a great influence on the ways in which flows occur (or don't).

For leaders what is actually flowing (or not flowing) through existing connections is of paramount importance. Flows shape how we interact with and influence each other.

Consequently, traditional logic will be turned on its head. The initial focus will be on what it takes to optimize the quality of flows. This will be followed by exploring how connections can ensure that flows are disseminated extensively throughout a system.

Improve the Flow Capacity of the Nodes

Nodes in a network are sensors that can receive and disseminate information and energy. Optimizing flows between the nodes begins with optimizing the quality of the sensors. The following example (Christakis & Fowler, 2009, p. 10) illustrates individuals who are fine-tuned to relay information and energy both quickly and accurately.

Military recruits join battalions of ca. 100 members. Yet they train in small groups consisting of no more than ten individuals. These small cohorts spend a lot of time together during workouts, deployments, and exercises. This mutual reliance breeds a culture of open and transparent communication.

Recruits learn quickly that individual actions can have a significant impact on their cohort's success (or failure). The relationships that develop are so strong that soldiers are willing to fight and die for each other. For most recruits, the bonds that are formed during their military service last a lifetime.

This example highlights all the issues that improve the quality of flows in networks: **bonding relationships**, **small teams**, **social emotional competencies**, **awe**, and **curiosity**. What follows is an in-depth review of each of these issues and their implications for leaders.

Build Bonding Relationships to Improve Flows

Edgar Schein identified four different levels of relationships (see Figure 11)

At a Level 2 relationship, a person conveys the fact that "*I see you.*" This is not necessarily "*I like you*" or "*I want to be your friend.*" At this level, a person lets another person know through their words, demeanor, and body language that they are aware of another person's total presence. In other words, "*I see you as more than a fellow employee, or associate, or team member, but as a whole person.*"

To engender trust and open communication,
Level 2 relationships are essential.

In most work environments, Level 1 relationships that are both dominant and/ or exploitative tend to prevail. Henry Ford is famously reputed to have said: "*Why is it that I always get the whole person when what I really want is a pair of hands?*" (Wagner & Harter, 2007).

In an environment in which Level 1 relationships predominate, psychological safety suffers and a willingness to share vital information is impaired. In a study that led to the concept of "psychological safety" (Edmondson, 2018), the

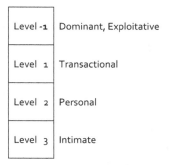

Figure 11 Relationship levels.[13]

---

[13] From Schein & Schein (2018), pp. 10–12.

doctor-nurse teams that reported the most operational mistakes actually para-doxically had the least number of accidents involving patients. The openness to admit mistakes led to operational improvements and, as a result, benefitted the patients themselves. This willingness to admit and report mistakes was directly correlated to the strength of the doctor-nurse relationships.

The quality of relationships makes a difference. Bonding Level 2 interpersonal relationships encourage the free flow of information. Employees are more likely to share information, updates, and insights with colleagues with whom they have strong relationships and have built trust. Both of these factors support the efficient dissemination of crucial information and energy throughout the organization.

Keep Team Size Small

The maximum number of stable social relationships an individual can effectively maintain is 150 (Dunbar, 1992). Most of these people tend to be merely acquaintances. Within this larger group, however, there is an inner circle of friends and family members with whom individuals maintain stronger and more intimate relationships. The size of this "inner circle" varies typically between five and fifteen people. This small number is a reflection of the fact that individuals need to dedicate a significant amount of time and emotional investment to maintain strong and intimate relationships.

The more people who are in a work group, the larger the number of relationships that need to be maintained (see Figure 12).

To act as an effective team, all its members need to be connected to everyone else in the team. If this is not the case, there will be multiple clusters of people working together but not one team. Correspondingly, the addition of another team member exponentially drives up the number of relationships that are required to keep everyone in the team connected. The greater the number of relationships to be maintained, the greater the probability of dysfunction.

It is easier to maintain a high degree of relationship quality in smaller groups.

It should not come as surprise that research results have confirmed that small teams consistently outperform larger teams (Hackman & Vidmar, 1970). Decades of empirical evidence indicate that the optimal number for a team lies between four and nine members. Individuals report the highest satisfaction levels in groups of four to five (Ridley, 2016).

Strengthen Sensing Skills (Social Emotional Competence)

Neuroplasticity and epigenetics – two recent breakthroughs in neurological research – have altered science's views of the ability of human beings to

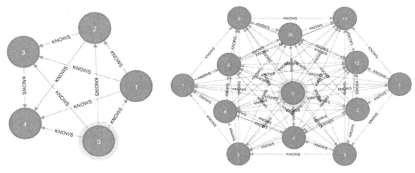

5 people, 20 relationships   13 people, 78 relationships

Figure 12 Number of required relationships by size of team. Image taken from Ridley (2016).

change and adapt. Neuroplasticity refers to the brain's ability to reorganize itself by forming new neural connections throughout life (Rugnetta, 2023). Epigenetics is the study of gene expression (Fridovich-Keil & Rogers, 2023). Research has shown that environmental factors such as diet, stress, toxins, and lifestyle can impact epigenetic modifications (i.e., if certain genes are activated or not). Regular physical activity for example modifies DNA methylation patterns[14] thus reducing the risk of chronic diseases such as diabetes and heart disease.

These findings have led some researchers to conclude that "core dimensions of psychological well-being can be cultivated through intentional mental training" (Dahl et al., 2020). The Center for Healthy Minds at the University of Wisconsin has integrated well-being research, cognitive and affective neuroscience, and clinical psychology to create a framework of four core dimensions of well-being (Dahl et al., 2020). Their research has shown that through mental training for as little as five minutes a day, individuals can rewire their brains and cultivate healthy minds (Davidson, 2022).

Well-being is a trainable skill.

The project Educating for Well-being (EW)[15] using the University of Wisconsin Healthy Minds framework was launched in Mexico in 2018. It is a collaboration between the nonprofit organization AtentaMente[16] and the Ministries of Education

---

[14] DNA methylation is one of several epigenetic mechanisms that cells use to control gene expression. Methylation is the addition of a methyl group (CH_3) to a DNA molecule. Methylation tends to repress gene expression.

[15] https://hundred.org/en/innovations/educating-for-wellbeing-ew

[16] www.atentamente.com.mx/

in six Mexican states. One in two children live in poverty in Mexico and 60 percent are behind in school by grade six. The EW aspires to break this pattern.

As of 2022, the initiative had reached over 12,500 preschool principals, teachers, and educational authorities and indirectly impacted over 300,000 students.[17] The focus is to enhance adult social and emotional competency (SEC) and cultivate adult well-being to build caring environments. The aim is to protect young children from adverse childhood experiences, and support them to develop healthily and thrive. Research has shown improvements in the teachers' and (even more importantly) the students' social emotional competency (SEC).[18] The EW was the winner of the WISE award in 2022, which rewards and recognizes successful innovative projects that address global educational challenges.[19]

> **Training individual and collective social emotional competency enhances the quality of flows in networks.**

Awaken Awe and Cultivate Curiosity

Awe is a feeling of *"being in the presence of something vast and mysterious that transcends your current understanding of the world"* (Keltner, 2023, p. 7). This feeling is often associated with once-in-a-lifetime experiences. But it can also be an everyday experience.

Awe occurs when people perceive the extraordinary in the ordinary. Awe can arise from experiencing a friend's generosity, watching a sunset, or appreciating the immense choice that is available in a supermarket. Experiences of awe open the mind and, by doing so, one's individual self gives way to the sense of being part of something much larger than oneself.

A research study collected 2,600 stories describing experiences of awe from around the world (Keltner, 2023, pp. 10–19). The following list highlights the distinct sources of awe that were identified in the research, listed from the highest to lowest occurrence:

1. Other people's courage, kindness, strength, or overcoming;
2. Collective effervescence (pride / joy derived from observing or being part of collective behavior);
3. Experiences of or in Nature;
4. Music;
5. Visual design (items from buildings to handicrafts);

---

[17] www.wise-qatar.org/project/educating-for-wellbeing/, see p. 2 "Future Developments"
[18] www.wise-qatar.org/project/educating-for-wellbeing/, see p. 2 "Future Developments"
[19] www.wise-qatar.org/wise-works/wise-awards/

Figure 13 Mandela walking to freedom.

6. Spiritual and religious experiences;
7. Stories of life and death;
8. Epiphanies (suddenly understanding essential truths).

The power of awe is manifest in the reaction to Nelson Mandela emerging from the Vector Verster Prison near Cape Town on February 11, 1990 (see Figure 13). People from around the world marveled at the moral fiber of this remarkable man. After twenty-seven years in captivity, he had emerged stronger from the experience.

The approximately 350,000 trekkers who complete the pilgrimage walk to Santiago de Compostella in Spain every year is another example of awe. These individuals experience collective effervescence. What might be regarded as a long walk through the countryside is transformed. Walkers experience awe when they are joined by fellow travelers who are walking on the same path that pilgrims have taken for centuries. This experience provides new meaning to Ralph Waldo Emerson's phrase "*It's not the destination, it's the journey.*"[20]

What makes awe so significant is that it is a trigger for curiosity. Curiosity arises when there is a gap between what we know and what we want to know (Loewenstein, 1994). A feeling of awe enables a person to become aware of what they don't know and therefore want to learn more. A famous example is the story of Isaac Newton's awe of a rainbow, which made him curious about the science of colors in the sky and ultimately led to his "*New Theory about Light and Colors*" (1672)[21]

---

[20] Ralph Waldo Emerson, Self-Reliance: An Excerpt from Collected Essays, First Series (1841).
[21] www.ncbi.nlm.nih.gov/pmc/articles/PMC4360081/

Awe and curiosity are the two sparks which ignite the flames of proactivity in networks, inspiring individuals to explore the unknown, connect the uncharted, and transform the mundane into the extraordinary.

Curiosity is the ultimate driver of learning (Ashcroft et al., 2020, pp. 213–215). Curiosity stimulates individuals to seek out new knowledge and engage with others. By seeking opportunities to connect with like-minded individuals or experts in their field, curious individuals proactively build relationships and partnerships within a network.

Improve the Flow Capacity of the System

Despite all that can be done to improve flows at the level of nodes, this is only part of the story. As much as the parts influence the whole, network science reminds us that the whole also influences the parts.

The metaphor of an electromagnetic field illustrates this point. This electromagnetic field is a **property of space**, not a property of the particles that comprise it. The field, which was created by the particles, has in turn a major influence on the particles themselves. An electromagnetic field shifts and **aligns** these particles so that they all face in a specific direction.

Resonance refers to the phenomenon of energy transfer (Brittanica, 2023). The energy in the electromagnetic field is efficiently transferred or amplified when it matches the natural frequency of a receiving system. An example is a radio antenna, which is designed to capture radio waves. To accomplish this function, the antenna resonates at the same frequency as the transmitted radio waves. This resonance makes the efficient transfer of energy possible.

What follows is a closer look at why **purpose is the electromagnetic field of organizations**. A well-defined and shared purpose channels proactive behaviors in a given direction and creates resonance among stakeholders. This resonance is embodied in the motivation, enthusiasm, and energy generated to accomplish the organization's mission.

Promote Pro-Activity

Proactive nodes actively engage in network activities. They initiate communication when needed, rather than waiting for requests. This leads to faster flows of information. Contrarily, passive nodes are relatively inactive. They are more likely to receive information than initiate it. A network with a preponderance of passive nodes can be unresponsive or slow to adapt to changing conditions.

Despite the evident benefits, **pro-activity needs to be channeled**. Proactivity without direction however can lead to unnecessary communication and a waste of resources.

Use the Power of Pull

Leaders and managers have often turned to Kotter's 8-step model when attempting to create change in organizations.[22] This model is primarily a "push" process. It requires considerable amount of coordination at the top of the organization to "induce" organization members to contribute to the change. This approach is typically integrated into a meticulously planned project with defined milestones and deliverables. Despite best efforts, this approach tends to be a linear step-by-step approach, which is often met with resistance along the way (Pollack & Pollack, 2015, Conclusion).

Such a "push" approach greatly underutilizes the strength of self-organization and the natural adaptability of networks.

A "pull" process on the other hand, frames the envisioned change as meaningful and desirable. It invites members to contribute to the process (Hagel III et al., 2010, pp. 1–3).

The nonprofit B Lab provides a powerful example of the effectiveness of a "pull" process. B-Lab's purpose is to build a movement to transform the global economy.[23] It started in 2006 with three friends developing a vision that business could be a force for good. With the introduction of the B Corps certification process, they created awareness for their movement. Companies that met high social and environmental standards began to be certified. As of 2023, B Lab has over 1,600 employees and has certified over 6,000 B Corps in more than eighty countries. It receives funding from philanthropic institutions, foundations, governmental agencies, individuals, and corporations.

Purpose is the electromagnetic field that creates the pull. A compelling shared purpose will:

- **Provide motivation and a sense of meaning**
  When people feel that their involvement in a network serves a meaningful purpose, they are more likely to contribute and engage.

- **Maintain focus and direction**
  Purpose provides a guiding principle for decision-making, setting common goals, and resource allocation.

---

[22] www.kotterinc.com/methodology/8-steps/   [23] www.bcorporation.net/en-us/

- **Act as a filter for network membership**
  Individuals and entities drawn by the purpose of an organization are attracted to engage and participate.

- **Contribute to the resilience of the network**
  Members are more likely to support each other during difficult times and find innovative solutions to overcome obstacles.

- **Provide a common language and framework for communication**
  Members can easily convey their ideas, goals, and strategies when there is a shared understanding of why the network exists.

Leaders can avail themselves of a highly effective resource called **engagement catalyst questions** to further encourage pro-activity in a network/organization.[24] These are questions related to an organization's purpose. By exploring and answering these questions, stakeholders can make significant contributions to further the purpose of the organization. These questions are intentionally not easy to answer. Instead, they invite members to "live the question," embrace uncertainty and avoid hasty answers. When well-constructed, engagement catalyst questions fuel both awe and curiosity.

The carpet tile manufacturer INTERFACE® provides an example of the effectiveness of this resource. Ray Anderson, the CEO, experienced an epiphany in the early 1990s. Despite all his success in growing the business, his company was doing irreparable harm to the environment. His insight provoked him to shift the purpose of the organization to include *"doing no harm"* to the earth's environment. A clear goal of Net-Zero Emissions was set. Anderson realized that everyone in the company needed to collaborate to achieve this ambitious goal. Consequently, the QUEST (Quality Using Employee Suggestions) initiative was born. The question of this initiative was straightforward but extremely difficult to answer: *How do we cut emissions to reach our net-zero target?* Ray Anderson provided all employees the opportunity to become personally involved. No matter what level an employee was working at, they were encouraged to help find workable solutions. It was a steep climb for the organization. Anderson called it the "Mountain of Sustainability" (Anderson, 2019, pp. 55–60). After twenty-five years of collective collaboration, Interface became a certified net-zero emissions company in 2019.[25]

---

[24] This is a practice that I have developed to deepen and activate purpose in organizations.

[25] www.prnewswire.com/news-releases/interface-announces-mission-zero-success-commits-to-climate-take-back-300949740.html

**Be patient toward all that is unsolved in your heart
and try to love the questions themselves.**

Rainer Maria Rilke

Summary

- **Improve the quality of flows at the node level**

  This is accomplished by focusing on the improvement of social emotional competence, the quality of relationships (Level 2 relationships) as well as fostering awe and curiosity.

- **The quality of relationships in small teams is superior**

  Research demonstrates that small teams consistently outperform larger teams. The ideal size for an effective team is four to five people.

- **Purpose is the most potent "pull" force in networks**

  It provides direction and through resonance transmits energy directly to the nodes.

- **Engagement catalyst questions encourage pro-activity and activate the purpose**

  These challenging questions are a resource helping leaders to translate purpose into action.

- **The catalyst for self-organization within a network is a shared purpose**

  A purpose that resonates with an organization's stakeholders provides the social field in which effective self-organization can emerge.

Connect People

A change in connections can have dramatic consequences. Take the example of the impact of reintroducing wolves into Yellowstone National Park in the 1990s.

As the wolf population in the National Park increased, the elk population decreased due to the wolves' predation. The decrease in elk numbers allowed vegetation, such as aspen and willow trees, to recover and flourish. Beaver populations increased as they fed on the new tree population. The beavers subsequently enhanced wetland habitats. These emerging wetlands provided homes for various bird species and aquatic organisms. Thanks to the beavers' activity, stabilized riverbanks reduced erosion and improved water quality.[26]

This example shows how natural networks are interconnected. Small connection changes can have a powerful impact.

---

[26] www.yellowstonepark.com/things-to-do/wildlife/wolf-reintroduction-changes-ecosystem/

**In an interconnected world,
a paramount obligation of leaders is to
value and cultivate connections.**

A change in the way individuals connect to each other can have a significant impact in our human world of organizations. Software development projects used to be done in phases – the so-called "*waterfall model.*" Each phase was completed before moving on to the next phase. This process led to long periods before a software version could be released. Project members including designers, developers, and testers often worked in isolation (Lutkevich, 2023).

Agile methods introduced the concept of cross-functional teams. Agile teams typically include technology professionals as well as business and marketing specialists. They work iteratively on small manageable packets instead of long development phases. This agile process helps the team to continuously deliver valuable features and rapid adaptations in constantly changing environments. The substantial reduction in development costs has also led to greatly enhanced customer satisfaction.[27]

It's amazing to be able to increase the effectiveness of human beings by as much as an order of magnitude simply by arranging them differently.

Nicholas Christakis (Christakis & Fowler, 2009, p. 8)

Make the Invisible Visible

Organizational Network Analysis (ONA) mapping provides a visual representation of the interactions among individuals throughout an organization (see Figure 14). These maps provide valuable insights into various aspects of an organization's structure, communication patterns, and collaboration dynamics.

Sociologists began in the 1930s to make graphic representations on paper of an individual's social links. Today, ONA maps are software-generated and can represent nodes (people) and their connections even in the largest of organizations.

The ONA maps deliver primarily two types of information: the **positioning of individual nodes** and the **structure of the network**.

The first type of information highlights the **positioning of individual nodes** and their potential roles in the network.

---

[27] For a more detailed discussion of Agile methods, see Section 4 of this Cambridge Elements edition.

Figure 14 ONA mapping of the University of Minnesota. Image from Bartholomay et al. (2011).

Central connectors are high degree centrality nodes that may serve as potential hubs. **Brokers** are individuals who bridge connections between different regions of the network. A high Betweenness Centrality is ideal for this role. Opinion leaders or **Influencers** are nodes with high Eigenvector Centrality.[28] By asking nuanced questions such as *"Who inspires you and/or motivates you to be more engaged?,"* ONA maps can identify **energizers** and **de-energizers** within a network. The ONA maps also reveal nodes with few connections that may be isolated on the **periphery** of the network.

The second type of information emphasizes the network's **structure**. The **Density**[29] of the network represents the intensity of members' connections. The measurement of the **Average Path Length** reveals the accessibility of nodes in the network. This path length specifies the number of steps that are required on average to send information from one node in the network to another node.

---

[28] For more information on the issue of centrality see Part 2 of this Cambridge Leadership Element, pp. 11–13.
[29] Ibid.

The average path length in many larger organizations is often greater than 6. From the perspective of six degrees of separation, the implications of an Average Path Length greater than six are revealing. Normally when "weak ties" are activated, the entire world is connected to itself by only six degrees of separation. When an ONA map depicts an average path length greater than 6, it suggests that there might be a significant potential for the improvement of communication flows throughout the organization.

Additionally, ONA maps reveal structures such as clusters, communities, and silos. All these structures directly influence the collaboration dynamics of an organization.

> **ONA can provide an x-ray into the inner workings of an organization. (It is) a powerful means to making invisible patterns of information flow and collaboration . . . visible.**
>
> Rob Cross[30]

It is important to remember that the map is not the territory. Context matters. An individual at the periphery may feel isolated or disconnected. However, being located on the periphery may provide the opportunity to focus on specialized tasks without being overwhelmed by organizational demands. Individuals at the periphery may also be able to offer fresh ideas and alternative viewpoints since they are less influenced by the dominant perspectives of the organization. Conversely, central connectors can be powerful disseminators of information or play the role of a gatekeeper that inhibits flows.

The ONA maps act as a mirror, enabling the system to "see itself." One might not like what becomes visible. However, when specific issues are identified, actions can be taken to alleviate them.

Dialogue sessions are essential to discuss the results of an ONA survey. First, they actively involve and inform individuals about the importance of network concepts and connections. Second, a dialogue approach helps participants to understand and interpret the findings. Finally, a dialogue can serve to identify actionable steps to improve processes, workflows, and decision-making.

> **Just the act of reflecting upon the results of an ONA mapping begins to change the connectivity of an organization.**

For leaders, mapping is ultimately more important than measurement. Traditional measures such as KPIs (Key Performance Indicators) and OKRs (Objectives and Key Results) are metrics that do not capture the dynamics of

---

[30] robcross.org (2023); "What is Organizational Network Analysis?"

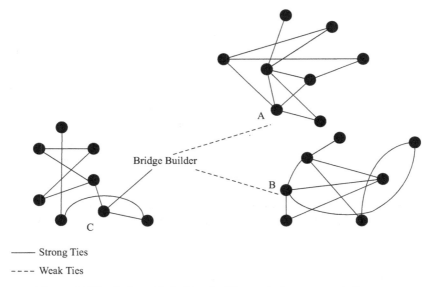

Figure 15 Depiction of a bridge builder node in a network diagram.
Image from Sozen H. (2010).

a system. Through ONA mapping, the nonlinear causality that drives the systems we live and work in is revealed.

Adapt Networks to the Task at Hand

Depending on what an organization is attempting to accomplish, different network structures are needed. In his book on *Adaptive Space*, Michael Arena illustrates this point. Innovation requires four distinct processes: Discovery, Development, Diffusion, and Delivery (Arena, 2018). To be successful, each of these processes uses different features of network structure and strategy.

> **Organizations are full of latent potential. To leverage this talent more fully, we need to shift our thinking towards the creation of different social arrangements.**
>
> Michael Arena[31]

Discovery is the process during which novel ideas and insights are generated. The key for success is building bridges between different parts of the organization and with the external ecosystem (see Figure 15). Siloed structures often inhibit this process.

---

[31] From www.linkedin.com/posts/michael-arena-21b6164_talent-activity-6553606396225605632-Mbau?trk=public_profile_like_view

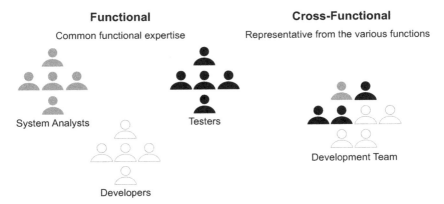

Figure 16 Cross-functional teams. Image from www.mad.co/en/insights/
building-cross-functional-teams

Bridge building can be intentionally strengthened through events such as large group gatherings. New insights are most likely to occur at the intersection of diverse groups fostered by such initiatives.

Development is the process where ideas are elaborated and refined. High levels of trust developed in a networks' cohesive clusters promote a proclivity to learn and take risks – behaviors particularly needed during this phase.

Cross-functionality is often a prerequisite in the development process (see Figure 16). Since trust takes time to develop, leaders are well advised to create permanent cross-functional clusters to support the innovation process when it arrives at this stage.

Diffusion is when a local innovation is scaled into the larger organization. Undeniably local implementation of an idea provides only limited value. If the benefits of the innovation are not sufficiently well communicated, important innovations may be dismissed by the larger organization.

Diffusion depends on energizers (see Figure 17) and their connections to help amplify ideas across the organization. These energizers motivate others to engage and take action.

Delivery[32] is the final phase of the process. In this phase any structural organizational impediments are surmounted, and the innovation becomes operational. New solutions are accepted and consequently incorporated into the formal operating system.

---

[32] In his book "Adaptive Space," Arena uses the label "Disruption" as the fourth D instead of "Delivery" as written here. In later articles such as Arena (2023), he changes the label to read "Delivery."

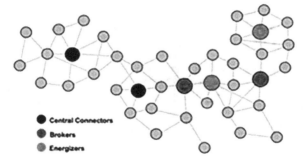

Figure 17 The type of role nodes play depends on their connectivity. Image from Cross, R. (Accessed September 8, 2023); Drive Organizational Change through Network Influencers; robcross.org; www.robcross.org/drive-organiza tional-change-through-network-influencers/

Decision-makers are often conservative. Novel innovations that are not sufficiently "socialized" (i.e., well communicated and accepted) may be rejected by gatekeepers. Network buzz created during the diffusion stage, the cultivation of strong Level-2 relationships as well as fully developed concepts play a key role in the acceptance of an innovation.

Arena distinguishes between two types of connections. **Bridging relationships** connect diverse parts of the network. **Bonding relationships** provide the trust necessary to enable risk-taking and learning. The following graphic (see Figure 18) illustrates the importance of each type of relationship and how they shift depending what phase the organization finds itself in the innovation process.

Spark Serendipity

Horace Walpole, an English writer, coined the word "serendipity" in 1754. He was inspired by the old Persian fairy tale entitled *The Three Princes of Serendip* (Al Galidi, 2021). In this fairy tale, the princes were constantly making discoveries of things that they were not looking for. The term serendipity is now used both for accidental findings in science as well as for the unexpected and fruitful encounters with people.

The famous story of the development of Post-It® Notes illustrates how serendipity occurs. In 1968, a chemist at the company 3M, Spencer Silver, was attempting to develop a super-strong adhesive. He accidentally created a weak adhesive that could stick to objects and be easily removed without leaving residue. This adhesive was considered a failure in terms of Spencer's initial objective.

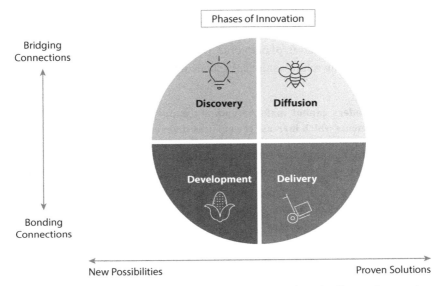

Figure 18 The role of bonding and bridging connections in diverse innovation phases. Image from Arena (2023, June 22).

Several years later a fellow 3M scientist named Art Fry attended one of Silver's seminars. Fry had been looking to solve a personal problem: he wanted a way to keep bookmarks in his church hymnal without damaging the pages. This chance encounter between Silver and Fry led to a partnership that ultimately developed the idea of Post-It® Notes. Despite considerable resistance from 3M management, Post-It® Notes were introduced to the market in 1980. Their use has revolutionized office work and personal organization worldwide.[33]

Serendipity is at the heart of innovation and transformation.

From a network perspective, serendipity is all about connections. Serendipity activates "weak ties," serving to connect different parts of a network that were not previously connected. When serendipity occurs, new perspectives unfold, which were previously unnoticed (Busch, 2022).

A personal experience provides an excellent example of serendipity. I attended a conference dedicated to the support of entrepreneurial start-up organizations. Hearing the latest technological and institutional developments was thought-provoking. Yet the highlight of my visit to this conference was an unexpected encounter. I participated in a workshop that

---

[33] www.post-it.com/3M/en_US/post-it/contact-us/about-us/

included several members from a tech platform. This group dedicates its efforts to develop Web 3.0 applications and blockchain technology to digitally support the formation of networks. Our mutual passion about networks has led to a working relationship and added an entirely new dimension to my practice.

While leaders cannot make serendipity happen, leaders can create environments which increase the chances that serendipity will occur.

There are many simple practices that leaders can initiate to enhance connectivity in their organizations. "Lunch Bingo" encourages employees to have lunch once a week with someone whom they don't know. "Peer Learning" (Beeson, 2021) involves bringing people from different functions and geographies together to learn with and from each other.

Conferences or large group meetings offer a natural environment for serendipity to unfold. Many such conferences or meetings focus primarily on expert presentations. While this format may be helpful in imparting information, it does not sufficiently promote the serendipity potential of such gatherings. The probability of serendipity at such events is substantially increased when opportunities are designed to promote ways in which people in the large group can interact with each other in meaningful ways. Conference and meeting planners should focus more of their efforts to offer interactive activities and opportunities for audience participation rather than solely on keynote presentations and panel discussions. Recognizing the potential of this approach, I have explored creative and innovative approaches for the use of interactive participatory formats in large groups.[34]

Organizations can encourage serendipity by regularly hosting large group interactive sessions. It used to be a major undertaking to bring large groups of people together in one physical location. With advances in digital communication, these types of gatherings can now take place on a regular basis either virtually or in a hybrid structure. With a robust design and the appropriate use of digital tools, these kinds of meetings are both interactive and results driven.

Convening regular large group meetings is like breathing. A system is oxygenated (aka "refreshed") by bringing large groups of individuals together. Project work is undoubtedly better done in small teams. However, when oxygenated, small teams take away new perspectives from the large group interactive gatherings. New ideas (and perhaps even serendipity) may influence how they then carry out their subsequent project work.

---

[34] See www.youtube.com/watch?v=dgVPJlb3z-U&t=1s

Activate Collective Intelligence

Computer programmers have a saying that " . . . *given enough eyeballs, all bugs in a program are shallow*." [35] Nowhere has this maxim been better demonstrated than in the case of LINUX.

In 1992, Linus Torvalds made the decision to allow anyone – at no cost to them – the ability to copy and improve the operating system that he had developed for personal computers.[36] The only restriction was that the individual programmers who made modifications were obligated to share their changes with the rest of the community. As a result of this decision, LINUX has become one of the largest continuous network collaborative development projects in the world. Over 15,000 programmers have contributed to the development of the software in the 30+ years since its inception.

LINUX was developed by programmers who received **no remuneration** for their efforts during LINUX's initial couple of decades. It is interesting to note that from the outset, LINUX was in direct competition with some of the most powerful companies in the world, notably Apple, Microsoft, and Google.

What has been the impact of LINUX's collaborative approach to software development?

- More than half of the world's fastest supercomputers ran on LINUX by 2004. All supercomputers ran on LINUX by 2017 (Vaughn-Nichols, 2017).
- Android – Google's mobile telephone operating system – is actually a LINUX based operating system (Tozzi, 2016).
- The financial world runs on LINUX. After the New York Stock Exchange began to use LINUX in 2008, most of the other stock exchanges around the world switched their operating systems to LINUX (Red Hat Enterprise Team, 2012).
- LINUX is the operating system of choice for cloud servers. 90% of the global cloud market ran on LINUX as of 2017. Microsoft, one of the leading cloud service providers runs most of its cloud operation on LINUX (Team Nuggets, 2018).

This code developed by software programmers in their spare time for free is now situated at the core of today's digital infrastructure. The multitude of programmers paid by companies such as Google and Microsoft were not able to keep pace with this development.

---

[35] Saying coined by Eric S. Raymond in his book The Cathedral and the Bazaar (2001). It was named Linus' Law in honor of Linus Torvalds.

[36] https://en.wikipedia.org/wiki/History_of_Linux

The power of collective intelligence has not been sufficiently mobilized in most organizations despite such success stories as LINUX. Ray Anderson, the CEO of Interface® understood this power. He was able to mobilize it to help Interface® become a certified net-zero emissions company in 2019.[37]

Collective intelligence can be put to use to deal with smaller and more common everyday issues. Beginning in 2010, the Italian government began to raise the retirement age.[38] Since that time, it has risen by as much as seven years for some parts of the population. The current retirement age is sixty-seven years for both men and women. During a program on "Active Ageing" sponsored by the European Union in 2012, the challenges arising from an ageing workforce were addressed using collective intelligence.[39] The purpose of this initiative was to identify measures in an increasingly aging workforce, to deal with issues such as knowledge transfer, workforce motivation, and continuous lifelong learning.

A meeting with ninety diverse participants was held in Bologna (Italy). The participants consisted of both men and women the majority of whom were over the age of fifty and were still active in companies located in the region. A handful of younger workers and retirees were added to the mix of partici-pants. Over a period of four hours, the group formulated dozens of policy proposals.[40] The most outstanding outcome was that policies that were sug-gested by the participants reflected the results of current research in this field. Whereas this group only needed four hours to develop these ideas, similar research results had taken years.

Harnessing collective intelligence is an art that requires that the following criteria be met:

• A diverse group of people are invited who represent the system;
• A clear purpose specifies "why" the group is convening;
• Well-crafted questions support the dialogue on issues that matter;
• Cross-pollination of ideas are fostered through active participant interaction;
• Output of the group is systematically documented and the results analyzed;
• Trust is cultivated through the transparency about results and the implications for the further use of this information.

By convening large groups either synchronously or asynchronously on a regular basis, the wisdom of the crowd can serve as a catalyst for further initiatives. Leaders may not only be activating collective intelligence to solve the issues

---

[37] www.prnewswire.com/news-releases/interface-announces-mission-zero-success-commits-to-climate-take-back-300949740.html

[38] www.statista.com/statistics/1174497/retirement-age-in-italy-by-gender/

[39] https://ec.europa.eu/social/main.jsp?langId=en&catId=89&newsId=860

[40] www.youtube.com/watch?v=3cypVn-Yf4w

that their organizations are encountering. These large group conversations also serve to spark serendipity and collective effervescence.

Promote Openness and Transparency

The book "Open Society and its Enemies" (Popper, 1945) argues that open societies are superior to closed authoritarian systems due to their responsiveness to change. Open societies emphasize transparency in government and public institutions, providing mechanisms for criticism and correction.

What works for society, also works for organizations. Over the past decades, research has shown that transparent organizations show a higher level of performance, learning, cross-functional cooperation, and a higher innovative potential (Stadler et al., 2021). This positive outcome is a direct reflection of unhindered flows of information, knowledge, and mutual trust.

By embracing open and transparent networks, leaders can:

1. **Minimize the blockages** that obstruct the flow of information and energy throughout a network and
2. **Create connections** that reveal new pathways for information and energy to flow.

Gatekeepers have the power to control the flow of information throughout a network. This control allows them to filter or censor information. This results in granting access to selective parties while denying it to others. The impact of a gatekeeper is exemplified by a middle manager who controls access to resources, budgets, and project approvals. This can stifle innovation through the quiet dismissal of innovative ideas.

Gatekeeper biases can also lead to a distorted or one-sided presentation of information that ultimately provides an incomplete or unbalanced view of a topic.

Transparency is the best antidote for gatekeepers' most harmful practices. Transparency compels accountability of gatekeepers' decisions and actions. It becomes increasingly difficult for gatekeepers to act arbitrarily (or in their own self-interest) when employees and stakeholders are aware of the gatekeeper's role and decision-making process.

Moreover, transparency fosters trust. Individuals are more likely to trust organizational leadership, (including the gatekeepers themselves) when they understand the rationale behind how decisions are made.

Leaders can promote transparency throughout an organization in multiple ways. Some of the options include hosting town-hall meetings, instituting an open-door policy, sharing data with stakeholders, creating employee feedback mechanisms, establishing whistleblower policies, and creating transparency in hiring and promotion decisions.

Digital platforms are further revolutionizing how organizations can achieve greater transparency. They provide centralized repositories for data and documents that allow for remote accessibility. Changes made to content can be tracked through audit trails and version controls. Blockchain technology can be employed to create immutable, transparent, and tamper-proof records in certain situations.

Leaders can further reduce blockages by promoting **bidirectional communication**, offering opportunities for both top-down and bottom-up exchanges of information. Information in traditional organizations travels much easier from the top of the organization to the bottom than the other way around. This results in asymmetric information flows in many organizations. Strong directionality such as a predominant top-down communication structure leads directly to a reduction in openness and transparency. Conversely, bidirectional communication ensures that employees' concerns and insights are heard and serves as the basis for more effective collaboration between departments.

Bidirectional communication is situated at the heart of Airbnb's success. Direct host-guest communications have led to a spirit of continuous improvement. Hosts and guests can participate in community forums that promote a rich interaction between Airbnb's staff and the ecosystem they serve.

Leaders support more open systems by being bridge builders.

A key role inside a network helps to create links between parts of the organization that are weakly connected or even unconnected to one another. Clusters and communities are natural occurrences in networks. When either of these groupings become isolated, they can become silos that are detached from the rest of the organization. Steve Jobs was famous for creating cross-functional teams that brought engineers, designers, marketers, and software developers together (Podolny & Hansen, 2020). He insisted that hardware and software teams work closely together, which led to a seamless integration of Apple's products.

Individuals at the periphery of an organization are poorly connected. This situation may have some initial advantages such as greater independence and/or fewer organizational demands. However, the people in the periphery often experience exclusion, isolation, and invisibility.

Leaders can mitigate some of the negative aspects of the periphery phenomenon by **promoting inclusivity** and encouraging networking opportunities. For instance, IBM emphasizes diversity and inclusion, not just as a corporate social responsibility initiative but as a strategic business imperative.[41] Part of the implementation of this approach in the workplace has been the creation of Employee Resource Groups (ERGs) such as Women@IBM, Black/African American Council, and Abilities in Motion. These ERGs provide support and networking opportunities for employees with common interests and backgrounds.

Finally, too much of a good thing can also lead to problems such as a person suffering from **collaboration overload** (Cross, 2021). This is a circumstance in which individuals (or clusters) are overwhelmed by the volume and frequency of their collaboration and communication demands. Collaboration overload occurs when there is an excessive amount of collaboration-related activities. Meetings, electronic communication, and collaborative projects all consume significant amounts of an individual's time and attention. This overload can lead to bottlenecks, a loss in creativity, a reduction in the quality of work, stress, and even burnout.

Collaboration overload is often experienced by top performers in an organization. This overload aptly testifies to how Preferred Attachment[42] functions in networks. The more value that is demonstrated by a top performer, the more projects and demands come their way until it is impossible to address all these responsibilities. Leaders need to be aware of these situations as they occur by redistributing tasks as necessary to reduce the load. In addition, they can act as coaches to support individuals experiencing collaboration overload.

Summary

- Connecting people is a **core competency of network leaders**. Network leaders are bridge builders.
- **Organizational Network Analysis** (ONA) makes the actual state of connections in an organization visible. The ONA provides a great platform to improve the connectivity of the system.
- **Dialogue sessions** to discuss ONA maps enable the system to see itself and often lead to changes in the connectivity of the system.
- The optimal **network structure and social arrangement** to accomplish a task effectively will depend on the nature of the task.
- **Serendipity** is at the heart of creativity and innovation. Leaders encourage serendipity in environments such as cross-functional teamwork or large group gatherings.

---

[41] www.ibm.com/impact/be-equal/diversity-inclusion-annual/
[42] See Part 2, p. 16 of this Cambridge Leadership Element for more on preferential attachment.

- **Collective intelligence** emerges if the interaction and energy of a large group is appropriately channeled.
- Leaders should **convene large group gatherings** on a regular basis. This practice allows the system to see itself, stimulates serendipity, accesses collective intelligence, and creates collective effervescence.
- Organizations with **unhindered flows of energy and information** demonstrate higher levels of trust and enhanced performance.
- **Transparency** is one of the best ways to improve connectivity in networks and remove flow blockages. The more information flows freely in all directions – top-down and bottom-up – the more likely an organization will thrive.
- **Intentional inclusivity** can ameliorate some of the disadvantages experienced by people located at the periphery of a network.
- Leaders need to be aware of emerging **collaboration overload**, by supporting the redirection of flows to other nodes when the situation requires it.

Focus on the Whole

The human brain is made up of billions of individual neurons, each with a limited processing capacity. When these neurons are connected through complex networks, they give rise to the emergent property of consciousness and higher cognitive functions. The brain's ability to think, reason, learn, and create is a result of the interactions among its constituent neurons. These interactions make the entire brain greater than the sum of its individual neurons.

This analogy of the brain is equally applicable to organizations. When individuals are well-connected, they can collaborate and create synergies together. Encouraging effective communication and collaboration among employees can lead to the emergence of new ideas, problem-solving abilities, and innovative solutions. These emergent capabilities would not form if everyone worked in isolation.

> **Network science challenges leaders to think systemically. A systemic perspective recognizes the interconnectedness of the parts and how this connectivity contributes to the capabilities of the whole.**

What follows explores the properties of the system that are not properties of the parts.

Strengthen Social Capital

Social capital refers to the value and benefits that individuals or groups gain from their social networks and relationships. It emphasizes the importance of trust, cooperation, and reciprocity within a community or network. Social capital can exist both within and outside of organizations. It encompasses the connections, norms, and trust that facilitate interaction and cooperation among individuals.

The following example highlights the role of social capital.

A community that launches a neighborhood watch group will be successful if they . . .

1. . . . can connect enough residents who have a shared concern for the well-being of their neighborhood.
2. . . . set norms to guide their activities. Some of these norms may include regular patrols of the neighborhood, protocols for reporting suspicious activities, and guidelines about how to engage with law enforcement.
3. . . . build trust in each other's commitment to the community's safety. This trust will increase over time as members follow established norms and act in the best interests of the neighborhood.[43]

Once a successful neighborhood watch group is established, the community has created its unique social capital. The connections, norms, and trust created allow the community to expand its activities as it chooses. For instance, it could produce a neighborhood newsletter, organize community events such as picnics or block parties, or even begin neighborhood beautification projects such as a community garden.

**Social Capital means
that a group has acquired specific collaboration capabilities.**

These capabilities can be molded and adapted for other related activities. For instance, if a leader in an organization wants to activate a collective intelligence approach to problem-solving, initially the norms of how this is done must be established. This approach builds trust via successful interventions. With this kind of solid foundation, a collective intelligence approach can be easily introduced as a means to address diverse topics and issues.

**Social Capital is the new gold.
Add value to others, value others and you will be valued.**
Lynn Ujiagbe[44]

Leaders who invest in social capital are better positioned to mobilize resources and to tap into diverse networks of individuals who possess different perspectives and expertise. This kind of social capital is invaluable for discovering solutions to complex problems.

---

[43] See www.nnw.org/start
[44] Lynn Ujiagbe is the founder of the Learnzone Foundation, the quote can be found at www.goodreads.com/quotes/tag/social-capital

Bolster Organizational Culture

The concept of organizational culture refers to the shared values, beliefs, norms, and practices that define the identity and character of an organization. It is the "personality" of the organization. Culture shapes how employees interact with each other, make decisions, and behave within the organization. To fully embrace network leadership, organizations need a "network culture" in other words, a culture that acknowledges the importance of networks.

> **We do not think and talk about what we see;
> we see what we are able to think and talk about.**
>
> Edgar Schein (2013)

Organizational culture itself is a network phenomenon. The law of three degrees of influence (Christakis & Fowler, 2009, pp. 28–30) tells us how values and beliefs spread within a network. It highlights a long-understood principle of leadership: what you do matters more than what you say. Being a role model for values and beliefs is an optimal way to propagate these unique characteristics throughout a network.

Organizational Network Analysis (ONA) is an invaluable tool to understand how organizational culture spreads as well as how to renew and reinforce it. It provides insights into the informal networks, relationships, and communication patterns that exist among employees. ONA maps can support the effective transmission of cultural memes and messages throughout a network by:

- **Identifying influential individuals** who could play a crucial role to drive culture transformation.
- **Pinpointing bottlenecks and gaps in communication** that may hinder the dissemination of cultural values and norms.
- **Uncovering subgroups or cliques** that may have distinct cultural norms and values.
- **Mapping the progress made in transformation efforts**. An initial ONA provides a baseline map of a network structure. Future ONA maps show how connectivity has improved and what progress has been made.

Reinforce Resilience

The robust flows of energy and information together with high levels of connectivity are critical elements in the creation of healthy networks. A further issue to consider in assessing the health of a network is its **resilience**. This is a property of the whole.

Networks tend to follow a Power Law Distribution[45]. Accordingly, hubs that have an above-average number of connections are typical components of a network. Hubs normally contribute to a network's stability. However, if they are too few and too powerful, these hubs can be a source of instability.

The excessive concentration of power and decision-making authority in just a few people at Enron (such as Kenneth Lay, Jeffrey Skilling, and Andrew Fastow) created a lack of resilience at this company (Palus et al., 2010). There were few checks and balances in place. Employees and lower-level managers were discouraged to question the actions of top management and dissenting voices were suppressed. This extreme concentration of power in one hub ultimately led to the company's downfall.

Leaders must be vigilant to monitor how hubs function within their organizations. The health and balance of these central connectors is where the resilience and sustainability of the entire enterprise are forged.

Contributing to resilience is **redundancy**. The human circulatory system exemplifies redundancy in nature. Organs and tissues in the body receive blood supply from multiple arteries. For example, the brain is supplied by both the carotid and vertebral arteries. This redundancy ensures that even if one artery becomes blocked or damaged, blood can still reach the vital organs and tissues through alternative pathways. The human body also has a backup system, which is known as collateral circulation. When there is a blockage in a primary artery, collateral blood vessels open and become functional to maintain the blood flow to essential areas.

Most business organizations today are designed for maximum efficiency, not resilience. Production systems that are based on just-in-time delivery provide a case in point. When properly functioning, just-in-time processes may lead to higher short-term profit margins. However, they can expose organizations to significant risks. Without a buffer of raw materials and/or assembly components, production comes to a halt if only one supplier is unable to deliver.

A similar issue is overreliance on one supplier. Prior to 2021, 80 percent of the mustard seeds used to make Dijon mustard came from Canada. A heat wave in Canada led to drought conditions in 2021, slashing the mustard seed harvest by 50 percent. Dijon mustard disappeared from the shelves from many supermarkets around the world for the timeframe of almost a year. With increased production of mustard seeds in Burgundy and other countries in 2022 and 2023, a disaster of similar proportions was prevented from repeating itself (Cohen, 2022).

---

[45] See Part 2, pp. 16–17 of this Cambridge Leadership Elements.

Redundancy is not a sign of inefficiency but a pillar of strength, which provides a safety net when the unexpected challenges of tomorrow test the current modus operandi.

Empower Emergence

Emergence is the phenomenon where unexpected and often novel properties, patterns, or behaviors originate from the interactions of individual components within a system. Managers in businesses who tend to think in terms of linear causality are constantly confounded by this phenomenon. For instance, a typical response to a squeeze on margins is to reduce costs by cutting staff. Managers are then surprised that laying off people leads to decreased morale and productivity among remaining employees. This dip in engagement ultimately has a negative influence on customer service and sales, which further squeezes margins.

Emergence implies that some of the outcomes from a transformation initiative may be unpredictable. Despite the best laid plans, the complex interplay of factors throughout an organization may lead to unexpected consequences or opportunities.

Emergence questions the traditional approach to change in a profound way. It challenges the linear logic of setting a goal, making a plan, and executing the plan. An organization seen from the perspective of a living system is dynamic, not static. Living systems are constantly evolving and adapting. This natural change process originates from what Dr. Fritjof Capra[46] calls "disturbances."

Disturbance is a natural and inevitable part of the life of any organism. It serves as a catalyst for change and adaptation. Living systems have the capacity to respond and adapt to disturbances, which can also be understood as "impulses."

That the origin of change comes from such disturbances, suggests that leaders from a network perspective should see themselves not as "change managers" but as "impulse catalysts." Such leaders realize that even small changes can sometimes lead to unexpected opportunities. *"Small changes in the topology, affecting only a few nodes or links, can open up hidden doors, allowing new possibilities to emerge"* (Barabási & Frangos, 2009, p. 12).

A leader who is an **impulse catalyst** embraces a **culture of experimentation** by starting small and testing ideas before scaling to the larger organization. Such a culture of experimentation (Thomke, 2020) requires:

- Connecting the experimentation approach to the organization's purpose and long-term vision;
- Working with prototypes to test ideas;

---

[46] Fritjof Capra, *Ph.D.*, is a scientist, educator, activist, and author of "The Systems View of Life."

- Using an iterative approach of continuous incremental learning;
- Encouraging "risk-taking";
- Providing resources – both financial and time allotment;
- Fostering psychological safety;
- Providing feedback;
- Learning from failure;
- Celebrating success;
- Willingness to pivot and adapt based on experiment results;
- Monitoring systemic changes.

Transformation refers to a significant alteration of an entire system. Transformation processes often involve moving from one stable state to another. The transition of liquid water into ice illustrates this process. According to complexity science, between these two states is the edge of chaos. Chaos is a state in which both stability and instability exist at the same time.

Systems at the edge of chaos are very sensitive to disturbances. Organizations entering this phase require leaders who possess a self-confident tenacity and a strong belief in their long-term vision. The stable state that an organization is leaving behind is clear. However, the future stable state that will emerge is uncertain.

The Swedish company Assa Abloy illustrates a successful example of a business transformation. Assa Abloy manufactured traditional locks for doors consisting of a latch bolt, cylinder, and key (see Figure 19).

Incrementally over the years, Assa Abloy moved into digital technology (Adner, 2021, pp. 95–101). Assa Abloy's vision had been to be *the world's leading lock maker*. With the shift of technology, its vision was eventually transformed into being *the global leader in access solutions*. Seen from this perspective, a key is not just an opener of locks – it is an identity and a symbol of trust. This transformation was not planned but emerged from continuous experimentation and a willingness to take risks.

Assa Abloy's business eventually expanded way beyond the world of locks. A good example of this transformative shift was their adoption of credentialing technology. This technology was developed to assess who gets access to a key and who doesn't. It is now used by governments to issue and manage official identification credentials such as drivers' licenses and travel visas. As a result of this and other innovations, Assa Abloy's business has expanded more than 10-fold. It is listed by Forbes magazine as one of the most innovative companies in the world.[47]

---

[47] www.forbes.com/innovative-companies/list/#tab:rank

Figure 19 Abloy historical lock. Image from www.assaabloy
.com/group/en/news-media/stories/access-stories/abloy-from-a-single-lock-to-
a-nordic-leader

Develop Systemic Awareness

Systemic Awareness refers to a deep understanding and perception of the interdependencies and interrelationships within a system.

Dr. C. Otto Scharmer[48] suggests that there are different levels of awareness, which range from surface-level to deep-system awareness. Surface-level awareness focuses on symptoms and visible problems. Systemic awareness, on the other hand, delves into root causes and underlying structures that lead to these symptoms. The concept of "presencing" (Senge et al., 2004) involves being fully present in the moment and deeply attentive to what is happening – both within oneself and in the broader system. Scharmer encourages leaders to shift their perspective from reacting to past patterns to leading from a place of awareness about the emerging future.

Summary

- **The whole is greater than the sum of its parts;**
- **Social capital is created when a group develops specific collaboration capabilities** that can be shaped and adapted for future collaborative efforts;
- **Network leadership depends on an organizational culture** that supports its principles and values;
- Organizational culture can be renewed and strengthened with the support of **Organizational Network Analysis (ONA);**
- The **health and resilience of an organization** depend on well-functioning hubs;
- **Redundancy** is not a sign of inefficiency but a pillar of strength;

---

[48] Dr. Scharmer is senior lecturer at the Massachusetts Institute of Technology (USA) and the founding chair of the Presencing Institute.

- Living systems can be disturbed but not changed. They adapt to the disturbances (or impulses). Leaders should view themselves not as change managers but as **impulse catalysts;**
- Impulse catalysts champion a **culture of experimentation;**
- **Transformation occurs when systems transition from one phase to another**. To steward such a transition, leaders need tenacity and a strong belief in the long-term vision of their organizations;
- A network leader develops a sense of **systemic awareness** and uses this sensitivity to lead from an emerging future, not from patterns from the past.

Leadership Metaphors for an Interconnected World

Leaders are often referred to as the "Captain of the Ship". This metaphor of leadership views the captain as the one who sets the course and navigates the ship toward a specific destination. The captain (most typically a male) embodies the ultimate authority. In this role, he makes important decisions about navigation, safety, and crew management. When storms emerge, the captain is expected to remain calm and composed. His role is to reassure the crew and guide them through adversity. Additionally, captains must show the ability to adapt to changing weather conditions and to unforeseen obstacles. Clear communication is important, especially in the form of a precise message of what needs to be accomplished.

This metaphor is so omnipresent that it may well prevail well into the future. Even in the 23rd century science fiction series Star Trek there is an easily identifiable "Captain of the Ship."

Network science invites us to re-examine and replace this dominant leadership metaphor. Two new and more suitable metaphors are emerging to take its place.

The Leader as Acupuncturist

Acupuncture is a traditional Chinese medicine practice that involves inserting thin needles into specific points of the body (Kaptchuk, 2000). Practitioners assert that the body's vital energy – Qi – flows through a network of meridians or channels. When the Qi's flow is disrupted or blocked, it can lead to illness or discomfort. Acupuncture aims to restore the balance of Qi by stimulating specific points along these meridians. Inserting needles into specific points unblocks energy flow, promotes the body's natural healing processes, and restores balance throughout the body. Acupuncture is often used in conjunction with other forms of medical treatment.

By taking a holistic approach, a leader – like an acupuncturist – recognizes the interconnectedness of the various dimensions of health in an organization.

An acupuncture session begins by monitoring vital signs such as the patient's pulse. Similarly, effective leaders take the pulse of the organization. They are great listeners. They ask questions, and talk to their people (i.e., "patient") to better understand any symptoms and emergent needs. They use this information to tailor treatments to the organization's (i.e., "patient's") unique condition. Such leaders trust in the power of the organization to heal itself.

The leader's responsibility is to stimulate the natural restorative abilities of the system. This is done by removing blockages that prevent energy from flowing throughout the organization. These interventions are often subtle, delicate, and precise. Such actions search for the areas in the organization where the most impact and the greatest release of energy can be realized. The ultimate goal of any intervention is to restore harmony and balance. This is the natural state of a healthy system.

Humble leaders – like acupuncturists – recognize that they do not possess all the answers. Leaders however will attempt to avoid invasive procedures unless it is truly required by the situation.

The Leader as Gardener

Since networks are the organizing pattern of life, using an organic metaphor to describe leadership appears appropriate.

A gardener creates and maintains an environment for all kinds of plants – from flower beds to trees – that is conducive for them to flourish. The gardener first prepares the soil, ensuring that the environment possesses the necessary nutrients for the plantings. Using both know-how and experience, a gardener plants assorted seeds according to their ability to grow in specific conditions. The compatibility with other selected plants is taken into consideration. Diversity promotes health in a garden. Monocultures tend not to be intrinsically healthy.

To allow each plant to grow to its full potential, the gardener makes certain that the plants get sufficient water and sunlight. Weeds and dead branches that can hinder growth are removed. Gardening requires patience since plants take time to grow and mature. During some years certain plants flourish while in other years they don't. Replanting plants is often necessary to provide them with more sunlight or to position them near other plants with which they are more compatible.

Gardens evolve and change with the seasons. Certain flowers bloom in the spring, others in the summer and fall. Gardeners aim to maintain a garden's continual sustainability, ensuring that it thrives year after year.

Just like a gardener, a leader
cultivates the "soil" in the form of social capital and organizational culture.

A fertile soil lays the foundation for the networks of an organization to thrive. Leaders constantly monitor the flow of information and energy to assure a constant source of "nutrients" for the system. Blockages of the flow of information or energy are eliminated as they emerge.

A leader looks after the people in an organization with care and compassion, acting like the caretaker of a garden. An attention to the whole enables a leader to develop a deeper sense of awareness via careful observation of what is working in the organization and what is not. These leaders exhibit patience, perseverance and express a willingness to adapt when required. Suitably network leaders demonstrate great **humility** (Schein & Schein, 2018), sharing credit and acting in service of the whole. This leadership style promotes a thriving and sustainable network throughout an organization.

Leadership Roles

What does a network leader do? David Ehrlichmann identifies four leadership roles that are indispensable to promote a vibrant, healthy network (Ehrlichmann, 2021, pp. 60–62).

- **Catalyzer** – *The art of inspiring action*

  Catalysts are instrumental to the formation of new networks and new projects. They obtain resources and foster opportunities to expand a network's impact.

- **Facilitator** – *The art of guiding network members to find common ground and collaborate together*

  Facilitators design and lead gatherings of diverse people, hold space for different points of view, and support the flow of discussions.

- **Weaver** – *The art of fostering new connections and deepening relationships*

  Weavers (sometimes referred to as Brokers or Bridge Builders[49] by other authors) connect individuals and communities with each other and inspire self-organization.

- **Coordinator** – *The art of organizing the network's internal systems to enable members to advance collective work*

  Coordinators focus on the optimization of information flows throughout the system.

---

[49] See Cross (2023) and Arena (2018). I prefer the concept of "bridge builders" since it emphasizes the importance of connection.

Each of these roles is not assigned to a specific individual. Any of these roles can be embodied by any leader within the network. An individual leader does not need to master each role. However, all roles are required for a network to thrive. This presupposes that in a network, leadership is shared.

> **Shared leadership ... is less like an orchestra, where the conductor is always in charge, and more like a jazz band, where leadership is passed around ... depending on what the music demands at the moment and who feels most moved by the spirit to express the music.**
>
> **Phillip Schlechty** (2004)

Decentralized AND Connected Leadership

A thriving network strives to optimize flows throughout its system (organization). This can be achieved by strengthening the capacity of the nodes to promote optimal flow. It can also be achieved by the cultivation of connections and network structures that generate new pathways for information and energy to flow.

> **The leadership function is decisive for a network to thrive. Leaders facilitate connections, build relationships, enhance social emotional competence, inspire awe and curiosity.**

For maximum impact leadership should be decentralized. As the rule of three degrees of influence (Christakis & Fowler, 2009, pp. 28–30) implies, leaders will have the most influence on the behaviors, beliefs, and values of the people with whom they are most closely connected. To maximize leadership impact, a distribution of many leaders throughout the network is advantageous. Decentralized leadership has the added benefit that it promotes inclusivity by granting a broader spectrum of members the opportunity to take on leadership roles. Decentralized leadership fosters a sense of ownership and commitment.

A potential disadvantage of decentralized leadership is that it can lack coordination and its leaders could consequently lose a sense of the whole. Seeing the whole is one of the key tasks of network leadership. Leaders in a network organization therefore need to be not only decentralized but also well connected to each other.

> **Network leadership thrives on the synergy of a collective of leaders.**

Connected leadership enables leaders to engage in collective problem-solving and decision-making processes based on their diverse perspectives and expertise. The "electromagnetic field" of purpose[50] becomes indispensable as a coordination mechanism to hold the whole together.

---

[50] See Part pp. 28–30 of this Cambridge Leadership Element.

High levels of connectivity among network leaders support a strong organizational culture and help to build social capital, promoting transparency and accountability. In addition, decentralized and connected leadership structures enhance the resilience of the network because it builds redundancy directly into the system's architecture.

Many organizations today still pursue a centralized hierarchical leadership structure where information flows primarily from the top to the bottom of the organization. In the following section, how the architecture of organizations is shifting to reflect and embody network principles is examined.

4 Ecosystem Evolution

One of the most dominant organizational models for over a century has been the centralized hierarchical business corporation. Henry Mintzberg named it the "Machine Bureaucracy" (Mintzberg, 1980).

His reflections on **the nature of a hierarchical organization** highlighted the following characteristics:

- Processes are highly **standardized and follow established rules and routines**;
- Employees have **well-defined roles and responsibilities**; positions are highly specialized;
- **Decision-making authority is concentrated at the top of the hierarchy**. This results in a limited delegation of decision-making power to lower levels of the organization;
- The organizational structure is characterized by a **clear and rigid chain of command**. Communication flows vertically, following the hierarchy;
- Interactions tend to **be impersonal and transactional**;
- **The primary goal is to achieve high levels of efficiency and productivity**; Processes are designed to minimize waste and maximize output;
- There is a **major emphasis on control**. Managers and supervisors closely monitor the work of employees. This ensures that their work aligns with established standards and procedures;
- The aim is **to create stable and predictable work environments**.

This model has been so successful that it is predominant in most businesses. Many public sector and nonprofit organizations have also implemented many characteristics of a "Machine Bureaucracy."

Like all organizations, a "Machine Bureaucracy" is a special kind of network that exhibits unique structural features. In a "Machine Bureaucracy," there is a clear top-down structure. This controls the power flow of authority and decision-making from the top to lower levels. When a "Machine Bureaucracy" is illustrated, it resembles an inverted tree-like network structure (see Figure 20) with the CEO at the top and various levels of management branching out below.

High degrees of centrality[51] are concentrated at the top of the hierarchy, which serves to streamline the decision-making process and control the flow of information. Even though information can flow in all directions, in a "Machine Bureaucracy," the actual information flow tends to be asymmetrical, flowing mostly top down. This is one of the reasons for the prevalence of silos in this type of organization. The emphasis on vertical communication and control hinders horizontal and lateral communication between departments.

The success of the "Machine Bureaucracy" is based on the concept of "scalable efficiency." This postulates that as a business increases the scale of its operations, costs do not increase by the same proportionate amount. The focus of this approach is to optimize resource utilization and eliminate all redundancies.

The "Machine Bureaucracy" has enjoyed remarkable success for more than 100 years. However, there are numerous signs that this model is struggling to adapt to the accelerated pace of change of the digital era.

The average corporate lifespan[52] has dropped from ca. thirty-five years in the 1970s to twenty-one years in 2020 (Viguerie et al., 2021). This lifespan is forecasted to drop to fifteen years by 2030. In a separate study (Hagel III, 2021, pp. 8–9) John Hagel identified that return on assets (ROA) for all publicly traded companies in the US declined by 75 percent from 1965 to 2019. Return on assets is a holistic way to assess company performance. It encompasses both income performance and the assets required to run a business. This measure captures the effectiveness of

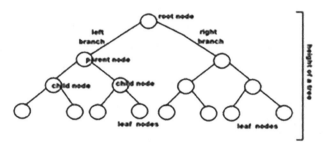

Figure 20 Tree network structure. Image from Sharma (2023).

---

a company to exploit business opportunities. This decline in ROA explains why corporate lifespans have decreased. To remain in business, companies need to earn a healthy return on their assets.

Why has ROA dropped consistently over time across all industries? Hagel concluded that the scalable efficiency model tends to stop **network effects** that create exponentially expanding value not only for shareholders but for all stakeholders (Hagel III, 2021, pp. 52 and 121–122). Network effects are blocked due to a top-down approach that limits lateral peer-to-peer and bottom-up information flows. These barriers prevent for instance, innovative ideas from employees at lower levels in the hierarchy to be adequately considered. This is one of the reasons why corporations often turn to start-ups instead of their own employees for innovative ideas.

Network effects also erode the viability of the scalable efficiency model itself. Cloud computing and outsourcing reduce the need for large in-house IT departments. E-commerce enables small and medium-sized businesses to reach a global customer base without the need for a large physical retail presence.

There are several **alternative organizational models** emerging to address these issues. These approaches demonstrate substantially different network structures and more optimal information flows than those exhibited in a "Machine Bureaucracy" model.

This shift in the architecture of organizations is an increasingly important terrain for leaders to understand. This transformation impacts how leadership is and will be practiced in the twenty-first century.

What follows are examples of novel organizational models. These models are examined in the order in which their architecture is influenced by network principles.

It is vital for leaders to understand the implications of these moving tectonic plates that are shifting right underneath their feet.

The Impact of Networks on the Evolution of Organizational Structure

Agile

A group of seven software developers met in Utah (USA) in February 2001. These individuals of diverse backgrounds brought deep experience with various software development methodologies. Together they drafted a document titled "The Agile Manifesto" comprised of four key values and twelve principles.[53]

This Manifesto was a response to the shortcomings of traditional plan-driven software development. It aimed to offer a more adaptive and customer-centric

---

[53] For a detailed overview of the agile values and principles see https://agilemanifesto.org

approach. Moreover, it focused on advocating iterative and incremental development, continuous customer collaboration, and the ability to respond to changing requirements.

The Agile Manifesto has had a profound impact on the software development industry. It has led to the development of various Agile methodologies and frameworks such as Scrum, Kanban, and others.

The use of an agile approach promotes self-organizing teams and the reduction of hierarchical levels. Team members have more autonomy and are empowered to make decisions collectively, reducing the need for command-and-control management structures. Agile leaders favor a servant leadership style (Greenleaf, 1996) that focuses on facilitating team success rather than exercising top-down authority. Agile often involves cross-functional teams that promote collaboration across different departments.

The agile movement has had considerable impact beyond the field of software development. Agile methods have been introduced into numerous project management processes such as product development, manufacturing process improvement, and even advertisement campaigns.

The Coca-Cola company provides a good example of the use of agile beyond software development. Its marketing department decided to adopt Scrum to transform their marketing practices (Agile Marketing Case Studies, 2018). They formed cross-functional teams responsible for specific marketing campaigns. The teams are comprised of marketers, designers, data analysts, and content creators.

The concept of sprints (focused efforts lasting typically two to four weeks) was adopted. Instead of planning entire campaigns months in advance, the focus was on producing a minimum viable product (MVP). Iterative sprint cycles enabled the team to advance and build up their MVP. Daily stand-up meetings discussed progress and challenges, helping to align the team. Feedback was constantly sought from customers and fed into the development process.

The result? The marketing department has been able to launch advertisement campaigns more rapidly. These campaigns often experience a better overall performance than the products that emerged from former traditional practices. Team members report higher levels of job satisfaction and engagement.

Agile fully embraces healthy network principles such as cross-functional communication, experimentation, nonlinear causality, openness and transparency and self-organization. While it is primarily a project management process, its impact has gone far beyond projects. Agile has shown that work can be organized in new ways. It hints at the possibilities of shifting away from centralized hierarchical organizational models.

Platforms

Platform businesses have been around for a long time. For much of the nineteenth and twentieth centuries, newspapers served as platforms to connect sellers with buyers via classified ads.

With the advent of digitalized platforms something fundamental shifted in the twenty-first century. Today's platforms have no physical presence – everything happens electronically. Whereas former platforms tended to be local or regional, today's platforms potentially have a global reach. Access to digital platforms tends to be free. In the past, individuals had to purchase the medium (such as a newspaper) in order to gain access to the platform.

Today's platforms provide search services to aid individuals to find the items they want, customize offerings based on user data, and in some cases pinpoint where to bring the products and services directly to the customer. Uber Eats is an example of a platform that offers all these services. Such capabilities could only have been the subject of dreams for historical platforms such as newspapers.

Platforms are the engines of connection. Uber connects drivers with riders, Airbnb connects hosts with travelers, and eBay connects buyers and sellers. Platforms have permanently altered the economics of connection by several orders of magnitude. Adding a new user or an extra transaction incurs insignificant additional marginal costs. Furthermore, digital platforms enable self-organization. They provide a space where users interact directly with each other without centralized coordination. Ride-sharing platforms, for example, enable drivers and riders to find each other without the need for a traditional taxi dispatch system.

Platforms challenge the very foundations of "Machine Bureaucracies" based on scalable efficiency. The traditional logic has been that size is the ultimate competitive advantage. Size should guarantee lower average costs as revenues increase. But digital platforms provide a pathway for resource sharing. This enables scaling without the need to invest in costly assets.

An example of resource sharing is Airbnb. This platform allows hosts to share their living spaces with travelers. The Airbnb platform provides accommodations to travelers in thousands of cities without having to engage in costly hotel construction. In 2019, Airbnb reported on average 2 million guests per night. In comparison, Marriott – one of the largest hotel chains in the world – had on average 1,1 million nightly guests.[54]

The dramatic reduction in the cost of connection combined with the ability to share assets, positions digital platforms at the center of a new network economic model.

---

[54] See https://irei.com/publications/article/airbnb-vs-hotel-industry/

Platforms provide the means for various participants – including users, third-party developers, and complementary service providers – to come together as an ecosystem to interact and collaborate.

Ecosystems

An ecosystem is a complex network of directly interconnected partner organizations. It creates, delivers, and captures value by accessing a broader range of resources, knowledge, and capabilities than any individual organization could access on its own.

Ecosystems are emerging everywhere. Pharmaceutical companies form alliances with universities, research institutions, and biotech firms to develop new drugs. Financial institutions and payment service providers collaborate to provide efficient cross-border payment and remittance services. Precision scientific instrument companies form consortiums to pool resources and expertise to develop expensive and complex systems. Companies in the food industry join sustainability alliances to reduce their environmental footprint, promote responsible sourcing, and address issues such as food waste and climate change.

The nonprofit sector has witnessed an increase in so-called **impact networks**. These networks bring institutions and other actors together to solve societal and environmental challenges. One example is the Santa Cruz Mountains Stewardship Network that connects more than twenty groups, including government agencies, land trusts, nonprofits, research institutes, timber companies, and an indigenous American group (Ehrlichmann, 2021, pp. 22–25). The purpose of this network is to "*cultivate a resilient, vibrant region where human and natural systems thrive for generations to come.*" Nonprofit organizations increasingly realize that a network ecosystem approach is necessary to address complex societal issues.

A key feature of ecosystems is the **multilateral interaction** of its members. This kind of interaction contrasts sharply with traditional business supply chains. In a supply chain, the interactions are strictly bilateral along terms that are predetermined in a buyer–supplier contract.

Ecosystems extend the boundaries of even traditional industries. Audi, the German car manufacturer, partners with multiple tech companies to enhance driver assistance systems, build advanced infotainment systems and construct real-time data exchange capabilities.[55] Audi is also partnering with their competitors BMW and Daimler in a shared effort to realize autonomous driving.

In the field of marketing and sales, Audi has built coalitions with various other organizations in the marketplace. These partnerships enable Audi to

---

[55] See www.audi.com/en/company/strategy/business-areas/a4nxt-kickstarts-innovation.html

provide services such as ridesharing and subscription-based sales models (customers have access a fleet of Audi vehicles on a monthly fee basis).

Audi has also partnered with electricity network power providers to establish an electric charging infrastructure, thereby entering the retail fueling business. Partnerships with cities are generating new urban transportation services. As a result of all these changes, Audi no longer sees itself as a car manufacturer but as a provider of mobility solutions.[56]

> **Industry boundaries are collapsing everywhere you look,**
> **and the trend is accelerating.**
>
> Ron Adner (2021, Introduction, p. xi)

Leading an ecosystem follows network principles. When leaders think beyond their own products and their own industry, ecosystem opportunities become tangible. Ecosystems compel organizations to examine their roles and responsibilities in their communities and in society. By enlarging the framework they use to look at their markets, companies become aware of previously unseen opportunities and potential ecosystem partnerships become evident. These partnerships become tangible when a leader asks the following key question: *What can our organization achieve together with other organizations which we could not achieve alone?*

Leading an ecosystem requires "*being watchful, being thankful, taking nothing for granted, and staying humble*" (Adner, 2021, p. 160). In an ecosystem no one necessarily has the overriding authority. Ego is often the biggest source of failure in ecosystems. Failure often surfaces when an individual insists on leading or orchestrating the ecosystem alone.

The impasse that can emerge from this attitude is illustrated by the case of Apple Pay. As a company, Apple is accustomed to taking the lead in all its initiatives. This behavior predominated as it introduced its "pay by phone" service – ApplePay. In this case, Apple has been unable so far to bring the key actors – bankers, retailers, mobile operators, and other smartphone manufacturers into an effective ecosystem alliance. Consequently, Apple Pay's penetration of the financial transaction market has been negligible (Adner, 2021, pp. 139–143).

Partner alignment is the key to successful ecosystem orchestration. Partners need to understand the ecosystem's purpose, value proposition, and their own unique role in the ecosystem. **In a world of coalitions, trust is key**.

---

[56] For Sales and Marketing see www.audibusinessinnovation.com/abi/web/en/what-we-do/CRM .html; for an example of partnerships with cities see https://auto.economictimes.indiatimes.com/ news/auto-technology/audi-partners-with-deutsche-telekom-and-city-of-ingolstadt-for-5g-tech nology/71420907; for example of electric charging station partnerships see www.audi-media center.com/en/press-releases/audi-adds-brand-exclusive-charging-stations-to-its-premium-e-mobility-ecosystem-in-china-14999

This alignment can only be achieved if two factors are in place: a compelling "value proposition" and a clear "value architecture" (Adner, 2021, p. 14).

A compelling **value proposition** clarifies how the ecosystem creates value. In combination with a compelling purpose, a clear value proposition creates the "pull" required to hold an ecosystem together. When the pull is not strong enough, ecosystems either dissolve or evolve into another form of organization.

A clear **value architecture** delineates the roles necessary to realize a value proposition. In a coalition that is developing a complex technology, various **roles** such as research, technology development, intellectual property management, funding and investment, access to facilities, manufacturing, data sharing and analysis, regulatory compliance, education and training, and so on. are needed for the ecosystem to accomplish its mission.

A role can, of course, itself be an entire ecosystem. For instance, the European Space Agency's contribution to NASA's Artemis moon mission is the delivery of the Orion space capsule. The Orion capsule development is in turn an ecosystem cooperative involving multiple partners worldwide.

Building an ecosystem from scratch requires continuous experimentation. The process begins with a **minimum viable ecosystem** (MVE). An MVE's purpose is to attract further partners by showing that the collaborative effort is viable. As subsequent partners join, the value proposition can be expanded and may even serve to create new ecosystems (Adner, 2021, p. 73).

The locksmith Assa Abloy provides an excellent example of this process. At the beginning, Assa Abloy merely replaced keys with smartcards. However, this solution did not allow the company to use the full potential of the information stored on the smartcards. To unlock this potential, Assa Abloy had to enter into the domain of the manufacturers of control systems for buildings and security system integrators (Adner, 2021, pp. 95–101).

Assa Abloy's quest to enhance their value proposition led to:

1. **Learning from failure**
   Assa Abloy initially created a platform that embraced open standards. This was not what system integrators wanted.
2. **Creating a minimal viable ecosystem**
   The next platform integrated over 100 system security protocols. This allowed system integrators to link mechanical locks wirelessly and to do so using their own protocols.
3. **Expanding and enhancing the existing ecosystem**
   Assa Abloy gradually scaled its ecosystem to include more partners, new geographies, and new services. It also enhanced the ecosystem capabilities.

One such enhancement enabled individuals to use their own devices such as a smartphone to identify themselves. This meant that access could be granted without a physical handoff.

4. **New ecosystem creation**

The newly acquired identification capabilities, enabled Assa Abloy to create new ecosystems. In partnership with government agencies, Assa Abloy entered the business of pure identity, which includes authenticating documents such as driver's licenses and passports.

An ecosystem approach contrasts sharply with the prevalent efficiency mindset of "Machine Bureaucracies". Ecosystem leadership requires an **alignment mindset**. Partners need to understand how their contribution fits into the ecosystem's value proposition. Transparency concerning how each partner benefits from their contribution creates the trust or "glue" that holds the ecosystem together.

The Silicon Valley Model

The rise of technology firms has brought the emergence of a new type of organization. Tech companies remain entrepreneurial – that is, fast-moving, innovative, and adaptable – despite growing to sizes beyond the bounds of a traditional start-up.

Until the 1960s, the longitudinal valley formed between two earthquake fault-lines south of San Francisco was known as a fruit producing and packaging region.[57] Its thirty-nine fruit canneries made it one of the world's largest fruit packaging locations. This valley seemed an unlikely candidate to become the most vibrant and influential high-tech center in the world.

Today, it is the home of an extremely vibrant start-up ecosystem. Since the 1980s, Silicon Valley has had the largest concentration of venture capital firms in the world and the highest concentration of high-tech workers of any metropolitan area.

There are many reasons why the high-tech industry established itself in Silicon Valley. One overlooked rationale is the leniency of California's civil code that undermines noncompete clauses. Workers in California are free to apply the knowledge they gain from previous employers without penalty. This laid the groundwork for dynamic networks fueled by an unparalleled free flow of information.

The entrepreneurial spirit not only exists in the valley's start-ups but is alive and well in the larger tech companies that have emerged from this fertile soil.

---

[57] This area was previously referred to as the Santa Clara valley.

The larger tech companies tend to be "semi-structured" with a flat and non-bureaucratic organizational form. There is a limited standardization of work processes and job definitions. Much of the work gets done by small highly independent teams, structured like a "federation or constellation of business units" (Steiber, 2022). Much of the structure can be quickly reconfigured and redeployed to pursue new ideas and/or projects. From a network perspective, these companies can be described as **entrepreneurial ecosystems**. This approach to management has become known as the Silicon Valley Model (Steiber & Alänge, 2015).

Dr. Annika Steiber identified eight characteristics (see Table 1) that differentiate a traditional "Machine Bureaucracy" from an organization following the Silicon Valley Model (Steiber, 2022, p. 26):

The Silicon Valley Model works best when it is closely aligned with the following healthy network principles.

- There is a strong sense of **shared purpose**.
- The **quality of relationships** matters.
- Work is done in **small teams**.
- **Awe and curiosity** inspire people to conceive and realize the next technological breakthrough.
- The organization is **open and transparent**.
- Information **flows freely** in all directions.
- Structures are **flexible and adaptable**. They foster the formation of new coalitions to address the challenges of the moment.
- **Leadership is decentralized and connected**.

The perils of straying away from healthy network principles are revealed in Microsoft's journey over the last twenty years. Under the leadership of Satya Nadella, Microsoft rediscovered its network principles and put them back into practice. This rekindled the flame of its entrepreneurial ecosystem.

Under the leadership of Bill Gates and his vision of "a computer on every desk," Microsoft became the leader in the personal computer ecosystem. It used the lever of the Windows operating system as a critical lynchpin to create a vast ecosystem of developers and value-added resellers. Microsoft continued its dominance in the emerging internet age by winning the first round of the browser wars versus Netscape and successfully entering the game industry with Xbox (Shah, 2019).

After this initial successful phase, stagnation and even failure began to creep in. Microsoft was unable to attract hardware manufacturers to adopt its Windows CE operating system for mobile phones despite its early and timely appearance in 1996. Even after the purchase of Nokia in 2014, Microsoft was

Table 1 Comparison of a "Machine Bureaucracy" to the Silicon Valley model

Element	Traditional model (Mintzberg)	Silicon Valley Model
Strategic intent of top leaders	Cost reduction and profit maximization	Innovation and growth
Primary focus of top leaders	Internal	External
People	Valued for operational competencies and experience	Valued for entrepreneurial qualities and adaptability
Culture	Emphasizes control, efficiency, and quality	Emphasizes adaptability, innovation, and speed
Organization	• Bureaucratic, highly structured, use of larger units	• Organic, semi-structured, and flat
		• High use of small teams
	• Vertically distributed decision-making	• Selective decentralization to local decision-makers, usually the teams; Decision-making
	• Power concentrated in higher levels of the organization	power can be temporarily centralized at the top
	• Internally generated innovations	• Innovation emerges from anyone and anywhere
Leaders	Act as Managers by	Act as Coaches and Mentors by
	• Setting direction and priorities	• Setting direction and priorities together with the teams
	• Instructing what should be done (and in many cases) how it should be done	• Allowing team members to define the HOW
	• Following-up and control	• Supporting the team if problems arise
Coordination mechanisms	Through the standardization of work processes, job descriptions, skills, and output	Through a compelling vision, culture, simple rules, clear performance, and evaluation systems that are focused on key priorities.
Automated communication processes	• Cost of communication is low	• Cost of communication is high
	• Information can be managed through traditional channels	• Automation of communication processes is required

unsuccessful in attracting enough app developers to this operating system. Consequently, it could not compete with Apple's iOS and Google's Android platforms (Kagan, 2019).

Microsoft's historical strategy of using its dominant platforms to become the arbiter of software and hardware standards had alienated both software and hardware providers. When new markets and opportunities arose, it was not surprising that Microsoft was approached with hesitation or outright hostility by key market players.

Satya Nadella became CEO of Microsoft in 2014. He prioritized value creation rather than a Microsoft-first approach. This was a key decision that meant that Microsoft could not and should not attempt to lead everywhere, all the time. By making this shift, Nadella broke with long-standing Microsoft taboos. He embraced the open-source software movement and opened interfaces and integration with rival platforms. Whereas his predecessor had conducted a decade-long war to kill Linux, Nadella declared: "Microsoft loves Linux" (Economist, 2020).

Nadella led a drive to find solutions through partnerships and new ecosystems. In 2015, this concept underlined the rewording of Microsoft's mission:

**Our mission is
to empower every person and every organization on the planet
to achieve more.**

(Bishop, 2015)

Until then, the fulfillment of Microsoft's mission was tied to the growth of Microsoft's suite of products. Nadella removed this constraint. If growth was accomplished by others taking the lead with their products and platforms, this was also welcome. Microsoft became more humble. Its entire purpose was now oriented around the effort to support others.

This shift of Microsoft's purpose struck a chord not only with employees, but with customers as well. Providence St. Joseph Health CEO Rod Hochman chose to shift the data and applications of his fifty-one-hospital system to the Microsoft's Azure cloud. His reason to choose Microsoft over Amazon, Apple, and Google was because "[Microsoft isn't] trying to be in the healthcare business, but [is] trying to make it better" (Adner, 2021, p. 173).

One of the greater successes in the Nadella era has been the rise of Microsoft's Azure cloud computing business. Nadella crafted a new ecosystem of critical actors to invest in Azure-based capability. As a result, Microsoft transformed itself from primarily a software seller to become the computational infrastructure engine, analytical partner, and AI enhancer for its customers.

By 2020, Microsoft had added over $1 trillion to its market capitalization since the beginning of Nadella's tenure as CEO. Microsoft has regained its place as one of the world's most valuable companies. Its stature has grown quietly and with humility. Its focus on building healthy network ecosystems and rekindling its own entrepreneurial ecosystem mindset has fueled this transformation (Richter, 2020).

Bureaucracy versus Self-Organization

The Silicon Valley Model is pushing traditional organizations to adopt more adaptive processes. The introduction of new management practices such as agile project management methods are attempts by more traditional organizations to copy the management innovations of the tech giants. But there are other organizations that are even moving beyond the Silicon Valley Model and exploring new territory.

One of the salient features of a "Machine Bureaucracy" is its bureaucracy. A large portion of managers in these traditional organizations supervise and control operations. What if an organization were to eliminate this bureaucracy? What if you could get rid of bosses (and gatekeepers!) altogether? (Hamel & Zanini, 2020). Some pioneer organizations are doing exactly that by successfully introducing self-organization practices.

Prior to 2006, neighborhood nursing in the Netherlands was organized as a "Machine Bureaucracy."[58] Regional managers supervised nurses in the field. To increase efficiency, norms for every imaginable type of intervention were defined and developed. For instance, nurses were required to administer an intravenous injection in ten minutes. To keep track of how efficient nurses were in administering services, a sticker with a bar code was placed on the door of every patient's home. Nurses would scan the bar code upon entering and leaving. Nurses then sent in forms that indicated which "products" (their name for services) had been delivered to the patient. In this manner, the activities of the nurses could be monitored and analyzed by regional managers. For the sake of efficiency, nurses were assigned to patients not based on any existing relationship with the patient, but based on availability, proximity and expertise (different nurse groups for different types of "products"). As a result, patients were taken care of by a constantly changing set of caretakers.

Jos de Blok was a manager in this system. He realized it was impossible to reform it from the inside. He therefore decided to form his own organization – Buurtzorg[59] – instead. Nurses at Buurtzorg work in teams of ten to twelve nurses – each team serving a population of about 10,000 inhabitants. These operating units are responsible not only for the nursing, but for all other tasks required to run the business such as finding clients, renting office space,

---

[58] See Laloux (2014), pp. 107–110 and Hamel and Zanini (2020), Preface, pp. xi–xiii.
[59] Buurtzorg means neighborhood care in Dutch.

recruiting new team members, managing budgets, and scheduling staff. There are no fixed positions. However, "roles" such as "treasurer" or "planner" or "mentor" are specified. These roles are not assigned to any one individual. They are extra responsibilities added to the main job of taking care of patients. Each nurse is expected to contribute to carrying out these roles as much as they can. Self-organization defines who does what (Laloux, 2014, pp. 112–124).

Buurtzorg employs today over 11,000 nurses and 4,000 domestic helpers. The nursing teams are connected to each other through a social platform named "Welink." This digital platform enables nurses to post questions and receive tips. There are no preestablished home care protocols. Teams are encouraged to optimize their operating practices by tapping into the collective wisdom of the network. Performance metrics of each unit are visible across the network. This transparency creates a powerful incentive for peer-to-peer learning and continuous improvement. A very lean group of 100 staff employees provides support services for the entire organization. Leadership at Buurtzorg is clearly distributed and connected.

Buurtzorg consistently outperforms its competitors. An Ernst & Young study (Diller, 2021) found that on average Buurtzoog requires 40 percent fewer hours of care per client than other nursing organizations. Furthermore, patients rate Buurtzorg with the highest score of all home care providers (Vos, 2008). It has also been named Dutch Employer of the Year five times since its inception in 2006.

Organizations like Buurtzoog that focus on and enable self-organization tend not to associate "roles" with individuals. This supports a collaborative team spirit and a sense of joint responsibility.

Another self-organizing company is Morning Star. This processor of tomatoes located in the San Joaquin Valley of California has no managers and no job titles. The "colleagues" who work there write contracts with each other, which describe their individual duties. Every colleague is accountable to their peers; however, no one is accountable to a boss.

The founder of Morningstar, Chris Rufer, stated:

> *We believe you should do what you're good at, so we don't try to fit people into a job. As a colleague, you have the right to get involved anywhere you think your skills can add value. As a result, our people tend to have broader and more complicated roles than is typical elsewhere.*
>
> *Everyone does better if they are free to pursue their own path. If they are free, they will be drawn to what they really like, versus being pushed towards what they have been told to like. The freer individuals are to explore those nuances, and to tailor their relationships around their own particular competencies, the better all those contributions fit together.* (Hamel & Zanini, 2020, p. 68)

The results vindicate the approach. Morningstar is the world's leader in the tomato processing business. It prides itself in delivering "demonstrably superior productivity and personal happiness" compared to its competitors. The company is also at the forefront of environmental sustainability in its industry.

Buurtzorg and Morning Star take the principles of network leadership to their logical conclusion. By eliminating bureaucracy and focusing on relationships, these organizations improve the quality of flows of energy and information. They connect people in unusual and novel ways, which encourages engagement, creativity, and innovation.

Nonetheless, skeptics point out that Buurtzorg and Morning Star operate in industries where many tasks are standardized. They argue that the nature of these industries lend themselves to a self-organizing approach.

This raises the key question: Can self-organization be viable in a complex industrial organization as well?

Rendanheyi – the Emergence of the "Network Organization"

Haier is a Chinese appliance manufacturer headquartered in Qingdao, China. This company disaggregated its once large industrial organization into thousands of small self-organized teams.

In 2012, the CEO Zhang Ruimin gave 12,000 middle managers a choice. Either they could join one of the newly created micro-enterprises and become an entrepreneur or be fired. Their current jobs no longer existed (Hamel & Zanini, 2018, pp. 85–102).

Haier radically restructured its business between 2005 and 2012. Prior to this restructuring, Haier had been a conventional appliance manufacturer with a traditional hierarchical bureaucracy. Over this transition period, the company transformed itself (see Figure 21) into an ecosystem of micro-enterprises (MEs), ecosystem micro-communities (ECMs), and platforms (Steiber, 2022, pp. 41–58).

Micro-enterprises are independent organizations. Each microenterprise consists of a team of ten to fifteen members on average. Initially, Haier unbundled itself into more than 4,000 micro-enterprises.

The people who work in these micro-enterprises are referred to as entrepreneurs, not employees. These entrepreneurs do not receive a salary from Haier. Their compensation is derived from the products and services that they sell to clients. These clients can be either end-users or other micro-enterprises within the Haier constellation.

The micro-enterprises are genuinely self-organizing independent organizations. They have considerable freedom to evolve as they choose. Micro-enterprises are responsible for their own P&L and can make their own hiring,

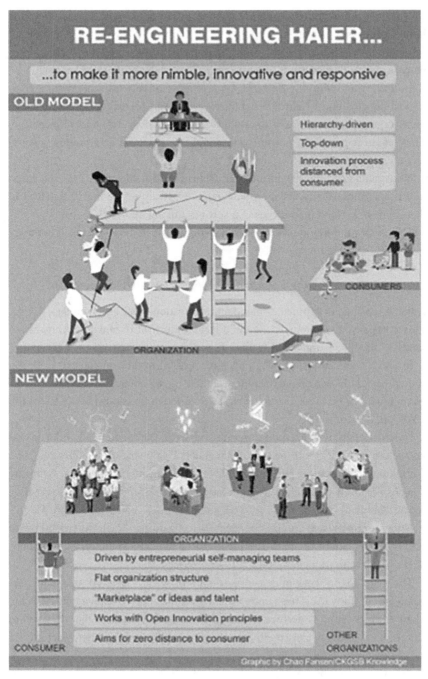

Figure 21 Restructuring Haier. Image taken from Fisk (2015).

investment, and resource allocation decisions. They can solicit outside investors – who can acquire shares in their micro-enterprise – to provide capital. Members of a micro-enterprise can even become shareholders in their own micro-enterprises themselves. Micro-enterprises can also fail. When they do not provide a competitive service, they can (and do) go out of business.

The Haier approach is an attempt to create an organization that mimics the architecture of the internet. The "Haier web" is held together by common technical standards (company-wide protocols and standard contracts) and hubs (ecosystem micro-communities (ECMs) and platforms) that facilitate micro-enterprise coordination.

Every micro-enterprise can contract with any other micro-enterprise. Most micro-enterprises typically have contracts with at least a dozen other micro-enterprises. These agreements are negotiated with virtually no interference from senior management. Negotiations are facilitated by so-called "presets." These consist of predefined rules for issues such as setting minimum performance standards and determining the share of profits. Once negotiated, an app provides real-time information on how each micro-enterprise is performing with respect to its preset targets.

This policy of openness and transparency permeates everything. Anyone in the organization can see how individual micro-enterprises are performing. Product development is also carried out openly. This allows micro-enterprises to determine whether they can and/or want to contribute to the development process.

Clusters of micro-enterprises come together to form what is known as **Ecosystem Micro-Communities or EMCs**. These are temporal alliances of micro-enterprises and external partners that work together to deliver products and services to its customers. There are currently ca. 400 EMCs at Haier.

EMCs are one of the primary vehicles for harnessing the power of the organization. The example of Yu Zhang illustrates this potential. He wanted to help ordinary people cook restaurant-quality dishes at home by using Haier's smart kitchen appliances. In a traditional organization, this kind of initiative would require the backing of top management. In the entrepreneurial world of Haier however, pursuing such an idea only requires the ability to set up an EMC.

Yu launched the Smart Cooking EMC in May 2019. To make this EMC a success, he needed to recruit partners. Internal micro-enterprises would develop new smart kitchen appliance solutions. External partners would offer the required cooking and food market expertise. He initiated the enterprise by recruiting four key external partners: a chef who specialized in Peking roast duck (a classic Chinese specialty), a food processing factory, a packaging partner, and a logistics partner.

Yu also initiated an internal Haier bidding process to recruit other micro-enterprises. He wanted a new programmable oven that could roast the duck with the push of a single button. Through the bidding process, multiple micro-enterprises joined the EMC.

With all the partners in place, an EMC smart contract was generated.[60] These contracts spell out what each partner needs to invest, the goals to be reached, and how future profits are shared.

After only six months, the Smart Cooking EMC successfully launched its first product. Three months later the EMC was already booking revenues of US$ 600,000. The profits were shared automatically with all partners. But this was only the beginning. Within the next year, the Smart Cooking EMC had expanded its offerings to another sixteen complex dishes that were delivered directly into user's homes (Minnaar, 2022). All of this happened without consulting or getting approval from top management.

> **The most priceless thing in the world is the human heart.**
> **To win the hearts of others, only exchange your own heart.**
> Zhang Ruimin[61]

Micro-enterprises can reconfigure their network of internal and external partners as new opportunities emerge.

A further co-ordination mechanism is **platforms**. There are two different kinds of platform in the Haier system – shared service platforms and industry platforms.

A **shared service platform** provides generic services commonly required by most micro-enterprises. There are shared service platforms for HR services, legal services, accounting services, and so on. The shared service platforms themselves are a cluster of micro-enterprises that have contracts with each other. No one is obliged to use these platforms. If micro-enterprises are not satisfied with the services provided by the platforms, the micro-enterprises can search for better solutions in the marketplace.

Industry platforms are hubs for micro-enterprises working on similar issues. For instance, there are product-based platforms for refrigeration and air conditioning. The industry platform's role is to be in service to the needs of its member micro-enterprises. Industry platforms do not tell a micro-enterprise what to do. However, they can function as facilitators to help the micro-enterprises identify opportunities and share best practices. One key responsibility of an industry platform is to coordinate major investments in technology and facilities (Hamel & Zanini, 2018, p. 139).

---

[60] A contract that is automatically executed once certain conditions are met. These contracts are coded into a blockchain that means that they cannot be tampered with.

[61] https://mingyanjiaju.org/lang-en/mr/7129.html

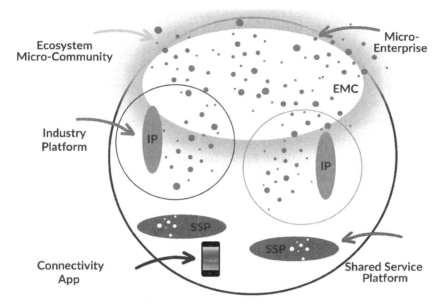

Figure 22 Rendanheyi organizational structure

Haier calls this system "**rendanheyi**" (see Figure 22), which roughly translated means linking employees to customer needs. A driving force in the realization of this model was Zhang Ruimin's passion to create "zero distance to the customer." He emphasizes that the rendanheyi model emerged not from a top-down decree, but from a long period of experimentation and learning (Steiber, 2022, pp. 41–42). Furthermore, the model is not static but continues to evolve.

The model's success is in part the result of a genuinely decentralized and connected leadership. When Zhang Ruimin retired as CEO of Haier in November of 2021, his retirement caused anxiety in the financial press. The press was concerned whether his departure as CEO might negatively impact the company. Ruimin scoffed at this concern. He noted that because of its restructuring, Haier had built a network of distributed leaders located in every corner of the organization. His own words give a fitting description of the nature of leadership in the company: "**Haier is a company full of leaders. It is leaderful.**" (Fischer, 2021). Zhang was confident that this leaderful organization is equipped to respond to any future challenges that might emerge.

The Haier model has been spectacularly successful. Gross profits in its core appliances business grew annually by 22 percent over the past decade. In the same time period, it has doubled in size with now over 100,000 employees. The company also created over $2 billion in market value from new ventures (Hamel & Zanini, p. 131).

In 2016, Haier purchased GE Appliances in the United States. At the time, GE Appliances was the fourth-largest appliance company in America in terms of revenue. Over a two-year period, GE Appliances aligned its organizational structure to reflect rendanheyi principles. With the exact same people in the organization but under the new rendanheyi structure, GE Appliances significantly outperformed its competition. By 2021 GE Appliances became the #1 company in appliances in the United States as measured by revenue (Steiber, 2022, p. 71).

Other companies have taken notice. Rendanheyi restructuring efforts are currently taking place at Bosch Power Tools and Fujitsu Europe (Quintarelli, 2021, August and December).

The rendanheyi model embodies every aspect of a **true network organization**. This model provides a window into how the power of networks will influence organizational development in the twenty-first century.[62]

Decentralized Autonomous Organizations (DAOs)

In the past fifteen years, technologies have been developed that can support and extend the rendanheyi model. This technological progress may potentially lead organizations to the next phase of their evolution.

The mysterious Satoshi Nakamoto unveiled the idea of **blockchain** to the world in 2008 (Magnuson, 2020, p. 9). Blockchain is a technology that allows for the transfer of value in cyberspace. A true transfer of value requires not only sending an item of value but also relinquishing ownership of the item. Blockchain authenticates this kind of virtual value transfer. The documentation associated with the transaction cannot be edited or changed in any manner. This guarantees the transfer. No third parties are required to legitimize the transaction. The transaction documentation is open and transparent enabling anyone to check its veracity.

Nakamoto's original software code laid the foundation for the creation of an alternative currency, based on peer-to-peer authentication. It does not require either central banks or governments. Soon thereafter the cryptocurrency Bitcoin was born, followed by multiple other cryptocurrencies.

---

[62] Holacracy is a groundbreaking system of organizational governance that emphasizes self-organization. This innovative approach aims to decentralize authority and decision-making within companies (Robertson, 2015). While it has been successful in smaller companies, larger corporations have been reluctant to adopt it. Several factors hinder the adoption of Holacracy by larger corporations. These include the perceived complexity of its governance and a lack of buy-in from top-level executives. From a network perspective, there's a crucial difference between Holacracy and Rendanheyi. While Holacracy retains all organizational functions internally, Rendanheyi acts as a platform unbundling the organization into independent microenterprises that are interconnected through smart contracts. Rendanheyi sees itself primarily as a network that happens to support self-organization, while Holacracy prioritizes self-organization, putting less emphasis on optimal network interactions.

In 2013, Vitalik Buterin realized that blockchain could prove useful in almost any online interaction. He embarked on the creation of the blockchain platform named **Ethereum**. He stated that it would become the "next-generation smart contract and decentralized application platform" (Buterin, 2014).

Buterin's idea was to create a blockchain for contracts. Unlike traditional contracts, Ethereum contracts are self-executing. All the provisions of the contract are contained in the software code itself. This is how it works: If a contract states that someone should be paid 10€ for uploading a certain document, the blockchain checks whether the document has been uploaded. With this confirmation, the blockchain automatically pays the sender the agreed amount.

Smart contracts eliminate the need for third parties such as lawyers to ensure that contracts are followed and enforced. They do not require auditors because all transactions are transparent for everyone to see. Once placed on the block-chain, these contracts cannot be changed or modified.

Banks have shown great interest in this technology. It can help them reduce paperwork and eliminate middlemen in many financial transactions. Walmart has partnered with IBM to create a blockchain food tracking system. When an outbreak of food-borne diseases breaks out, it can take days, if not weeks, to determine the source of the contaminated food. With the blockchain system in place, the amount of time to find the source has been cut down to 2.2 seconds. Furthermore, mass destruction of produce is avoided because the source of the affected items can be directly identified.[63] Haier has begun to use smart contracts in its agreements between micro-enterprises and as part of the formation and establishment of ecosystem micro-communities. Further developments are opening up even more possibilities.

Buterin coined the phrase "decentralized autonomous organization" (DAO) (Minaev, 2023). A DAO is an organization that is built on a blockchain platform. It has access to smart contracts and the ability to create its own cryptocurrency.

New blockchain platforms such as EOS have been inspired by this new opportunity.[64] EOS developed a blockchain platform to directly address this virtual space. Some of the innovations EOS has introduced include (Conti, 2022):

- **Free transactions for end-users**
  Users don't pay transaction fees when interacting with blockchain applications.

- **Open-source development**
  Outside developers can develop platform applications in multiple programming languages.

---

[63] See www.hyperledger.org/case-studies/walmart-case-study   [64] EOS was created in 2018.

- **Hightened transaction speed**

  EOS generates a block approximately every 0,5 seconds, compared to
  10 minutes for every block at Bitcoin.

EOS has also directly addressed the issue of energy usage, which has plagued
Bitcoin and other early cryptocurrencies. Energy efficient processes for valid-
ating transactions and creating new blocks have been introduced. The energy
use for this new platform is a fraction of what is required by the Bitcoin
blockchain.

These advances in blockchain technology have made it possible for existing
organizations to consider a DAO as a way of organizing their activities and
businesses. The HYPHA DAO platform[65] that runs on the EOS blockchain
launched the Beta-version of its platform in October 2023. Ensemble Enabler is
collaborating with HYPHA to understand and advance this new technological
development for organizations.

DAOs are not legal entities like traditional organizations. They exist as
software code. DAOs do not need to be recognized and regulated by the legal
system. Anyone can set up a DAO without incurring legal and registration fees.

DAOs provide an ideal vehicle for self-organizing teams. There is an
inherent environment of complete transparency. DAO members themselves
establish the governance rules that are upheld and executed via a smart
contract. Anyone can view and verify a decision or transaction that a DAO
has undertaken.

The roles that are required for the functioning of an individual DAO are defined
by its members. People do not have titles. Everyone is invited to contribute in
filling out those roles. There are no bosses.

The boundaries of DAOs are more permeable than in traditional organizations.
Anyone can become a member of a DAO if they have a computer connection.
Neither work permits nor residency papers are required. A member of a DAO is
automatically also a member of the DAO network. Given the transparency of the
network, a person can view and follow the activities of other DAOs. Transferring
from one DAO to another does not require a legal work contract. Such a decision
can be decided on the spot. An agreement between the parties only needs to be in
accordance with the terms that are written into and enforced by the software code
of the DAO.

An ecosystem of DAOs is formed by DAOs joining other DAOs towards
fulfilling a common pursuit. The governing rules of a newly created ecosystem
is codified and documented through smart contracts.

---

[65] https://hypha.earth/

The vision of the HYPHA blockchain network is to transform the way that human beings collaborate. It strives to transcend our prevailing understanding of organizations. The DAO world is currently in the very early stages of development. However, a glimpse of things to come for self-organizing teams and network organizations is becoming tangible.

The Network Tectonic Plate Shift

Many organizations describe the situation they face with the acronym V.U.C.A.[66] (Volatile, Uncertain, Complex, Ambiguous). V.U.C.A. represents the turbulence that they are currently experiencing. Organizations are searching for a way toward calmer waters, but the pathway to get there is elusive.

The turbulence many organizations are experiencing can be explained by network science. It is the result of a decrease in the cost of **connection** and an increase in the volume and the speed of the **flow of information**. There has been an increase by several orders of magnitude and it continues to escalate exponentially.

As turbulence increases, an acute awareness of the deficiencies of current organizational models grows. The traditional organizational model is not equipped to effectively handle the logic of networks. Both the use of Agile Methods and the creation of DAOs are evidence of the search for **network responses** to the challenges that organizations face today.

This radical shift requires leaders to adopt a new mindset. Leaders can leave V.U.C.A. behind, by adopting a network mindset. This mindset is the key to access a W.I.S.E. (Whole, Interconnected, Systemic, Energized) world instead (Beeson, 2023). W.I.S.E. is a domain where the primacy of networks as an organizing principle is fully embraced. With the transformation from V.U.C.A. to W.I.S.E., turbulence and uncertainty will give way to the stability of healthy networks.

The raîson-d'être of leadership in this emerging W.I.S.E. world is explored in the next section.

5 Homeostasis, Regeneration, and Symbiosis

The question about "What is leadership for?" has been a fundamental inquiry throughout human history. As long as humans have lived in groups, leadership and its purpose has been a subject of contemplation and discussion. One of the oldest texts in recorded human history – an inscription from Ptahhotep from ancient Egypt[67] – provides guidance on ethical behavior, wisdom, and leadership.

---

[66] The term was coined in Bennis & Nanus (1985).
[67] Ptahhotep was a vizier of ancient Egypt in the twenty-fourth century BCE.

Reflections on the why of leadership continue to be written to the present day. These modern leadership theories offer diverse perspectives to explain the raîson-d'être for leadership. These reflections range from the need to achieve specific tasks and goals (Drucker, 1974) to inspiring positive change (Sinek, 2011), to developing followers (Greenleaf, 1996), to serving the greater good (Kouzes & Posner, 2022).

This inquiry has focused so far on what leaders **do**. From a network perspective, these behaviors include improving flows, connecting people, encouraging strong bonding relationships, enhancing social capital, securing resilience, facilitating serendipity, accessing collective intelligence, empowering engagement through the power of pull, promoting openness and transparency, enabling emergence . . . to name quite a few.

Yet the age-old question remains, what is the raîson-d'être of leadership? Does network science provide new insights into this long-standing reflection?

Nature offers remarkable insights on the role of networks. The healthier each component of a network is, the better the network will function for all of these components as a whole. Think of a healthy coral reef.

The health of a social network is correlated to the quality of the connections and flows between people throughout the network. From this perspective, the preeminent pursuit of leaders in a human social network is to ensure the network's overall **health**.

Time plays an important role in the cultivation of a healthy network. The stability of a network is an issue that refers to a specific moment of time. This focused moment can be understood as a state of BEING. However, as time progresses and conditions change, the focus shifts to the ability of a network to adapt to the environmental conditions that encompass it. In this case, both the passage of time and the change in environmental conditions prioritize a focus on a state of BECOMING.

Leaders are compelled to effectively address the inherent tensions arising from these two dimensions – Being and Becoming – which co-exist simultaneously.

BEING

Ecosystem Homeostasis

The natural world provides helpful illustrations of a network's capacity to retain its stability at a specific moment in time. For example, the world's largest coral reef system is the Great Barrier Reef of Australia. The health of this ecosystem

Figure 23 Crown-of-thorns starfish. Image from https://daily.jstor.org/when-crown-of-thorns-starfish-attack/

has suffered in recent years due to the deterioration of the quality of the network that surrounds it.

Coral reefs are highly sensitive ecosystems that depend on a delicate balance of environmental factors. The health of coral reefs is closely tied to the quality of the water of its surrounding ecosystem. Declining water quality is caused not only by climate change but also in combination with human activities such as agricultural runoff and coastal development. A 2020 study estimates that nearly half of the Great Barrier Reef's coral cover has been lost since 1995 (Dietzel et al., 2020).

This declining water quality has led to a loss of healthy coral throughout the ecosystem and reduced the shelter, breeding sites, and foraging grounds for many species. Consequently, biodiversity has decreased. Moreover, the chemical imbalances in the water caused by agricultural runoff have led to an outburst of the population of a voracious coral predator – crown-of-thorns starfish (see Figure 23). These starfish spread over the reefs not unlike a cancer and increase the vulnerability of the entire ecosystem (MacDonald, 2018).

The stability of an ecosystem in each moment (Being) depends on environmental parameters remaining within a certain range. For a coral reef some of those parameters include biodiversity, nutrient cycling, energy flow, and chemical stability (e.g., temperature, salinity, pH). Changes in these parameters disrupt the balance of the reef ecosystem.

Homeostasis[68] is a biological concept that refers to an organism's ability to maintain a stable internal environment despite the changes that are occurring externally. Homeostasis is a state of dynamic equilibrium. It regulates various physiological variables within a limited range to ensure the optimal functioning

---

[68] See www.britannica.com/science/homeostasis

of the organism. In humans, homeostasis plays a role in the regulation of our body temperature within a specific temperature range. Homeostatic processes also regulate our blood sugar levels, blood pressure, the pH balance of bodily fluids, electrolyte balance, and so on.

Although homeostasis is a concept usually associated with individual organisms, it can be extended to ecosystems such as coral reefs as well. In the context of ecosystems, the concept is referred to as **"ecological homeostasis"** (Paradise & Campbell, 2016).

A homeostatic system contains two main components: receptors and effectors. **Receptors** serve to detect changes in the internal environment. These are typically groups of cells that respond to specific stimuli such as changes in temperature. **Effectors** are structures that serve to return the internal environment to its optimal state. This can take the form of muscles, glands, or other organs that respond to the detected changes. When a person's body temperature rises above a certain point, effectors such as sweat glands are activated to cool the body.

The health of the organism or ecosystem suffers when the environmental parameters are no longer within an optimal range. Diabetes for instance occurs in a human body when blood sugars are no longer at the right levels. Coral bleaching takes place when water temperatures rise above certain levels.

A key aspect of the promotion and maintenance of favorable health conditions is the system's ability (whether it be an organism or ecosystem) to regulate and restore balance through homeostatic processes.

Sense and Respond

The stability of a human organization therefore depends on the ability of the organization's members to **sense** significant changes in its internal environment and its ability to **respond** to these signals and return the organization to an optimal state.

In the context of a coral reef, the changes detected might be lower pH levels in the water. In an organizational context, such internal signals might be an increase in the number of employee sick days, a reduction in customer lead conversions or some other similar change that indicates an imbalance.

When an organization detects such imbalances, the key issue is whether it can respond and reestablish a state of equilibrium. A coral reef can respond to a certain range of pH reduction through various processes. Corals can change the composition and structure of their skeletons. Mollusks and crustaceans in the reef can also adapt certain internal cellular processes. The types and numbers of species in the reef can shift to favor those species that have a greater resilience to a lower pH level.

What does this process of sense and respond look like in a human organization?

Sensing the signals in an organization is the first step to the maintenance of its stability. Nevertheless, detecting but not responding to the signals received will eventually damage the health of the organization.

Blockbuster – an American video rental company – offers an illustrative example of the impact of sensing but not responding (Millegan et al., 2018).

Blockbuster's business model relied heavily on collecting late fees from the video returns of their customers. This practice fueled Blockbuster's financial viability but generated customer dissatisfaction. Blockbuster was aware of the negative impact of the late fees. However, it was incapable of changing its business model, even when its competitor Netflix made a major change in their approach. Netflix eliminated late fees altogether and introduced a subscription-based model.[69]

Ultimately Blockbuster was unable to respond to the signals that they received. When online streaming technology became available, the inability of Blockbusters leaders to sense and respond predisposed the company for failure.

A key role of leadership is to support a network's ability to sense and respond. The kind of internal signals that Blockbuster ignored were indicators that the health of the organization – and the viability of the company – was at risk.

The ability of an organization to sense and respond to changes in its environment is directly related to the health of its networks.

When online streaming appeared, Blockbuster's management was reluctant to invest in the new technology while its business model was still generating substantial revenue. Employees knew that online streaming was a game changer, but top management did not react appropriately. Despite the signals emanating from the marketplace, decision-makers at the company underestimated the speed at which consumers would embrace digital alternatives. Blockbuster's earlier inability to respond to market signals was once again made manifest. This time however, the company did not survive.

The story of the company Blockbuster echoes the situation of countless other organizations. Many such organizations are neither aware (sense) nor can adjust (respond) to the threats that they encounter.

Healthy social networks ensure that an organization is able to detect disturbances and return the organization to a state of homeostasis.

---

[69] This was **before** Netflix adopted online streaming.

An organization's most important asset is its social networks. Healthy social networks not only can collectively sense emergent changes but are also capable of responding with creative solutions to a disruptive environment.

Circularity

The degree of interconnectedness is a key factor in the health of networks. The ultimate form of connectivity occurs when the system connects with itself. A self-connected network is referred to as a circular network.

In a circular network in nature, one species' waste is another species' food. For example: plants convert sunlight into energy and organic matter. Herbivores eat these plants and produce waste in the form of feces and detritus. Bacteria and fungi break down the organic matter in the herbivores' waste and return nutrients back into the environment. The circle is closed when the nutrients (in the form of nitrogen and phosphorus) provide the essential components for the plants' growth.

Circularity promotes resource efficiency and reduces waste, thereby contributing to the maintenance of homeostasis in all living organisms and in the ecosystem itself.

An ultimate goal of network leadership is unquestionably to establish circular networks. At the level of society, this implies the creation of a circular economy that will optimize the stability and health of human society.

BECOMING

Becoming is the process of transitioning from one state of homeostasis to a new state of homeostasis. Leaders help to guide and support this transition.

Regeneration

Regeneration – narrowly defined – is the process by which life restores a system to its previous state after it has been injured or impaired.[70] There are miraculous examples of this process in the natural world all around us. When flatworms are cut in two, they are able to grow back all of their missing parts. This cutting of the flatworm results not in one, but in two flatworms (Bartscherer, 2014).

Without regeneration there would not be life. The sustainment of an organism depends upon the continuous turnover and renewal of all its tissues and organs. In a human body, 1 percent of cells are replaced daily.[71]

---

[70] Merriam-Webster definition of regeneration reads as follows: renewal or restoration of a body, bodily part, or biological system (such as a forest) after injury or as a normal process.

[71] See www.britannica.com/science/regeneration-biology

Organizations can also be viewed from the perspective of regeneration. Organizations are constantly renewing themselves, even as they function in a stable state of homeostasis. Renewal in organizations occurs in various forms from recruiting to training to succession planning. If the organization is healthy – when disturbances occur – regenerative processes will restore its homeostatic stability.

Regeneration also allows for mutations (Maienschein & MacCord, 2022). The renewal of forests through wildfires illustrates this process. Wildfires clear away dead vegetation and recycle nutrients back into the soil. Whereas the forest does eventually recover, the postfire forest may differ from the original forest. Alterations often occur in the distribution of plant species, the structure of the forest, and its overall biodiversity. This process it is called **ecological succession**.[72] A postfire forest typically exhibits a different structural configuration and a different composition of species.

Like a wildfire that devastates a forest, the introduction of e-commerce has had a similar impact on traditional brick-and-mortar retailers. Many traditional retailers experienced reduced foot traffic into their stores and declining sales as e-commerce platforms like Amazon became prevalent. Due to the impact of digital sales channels, many retailers closed some of their brick-and-mortar retail outlets.

Those organizations that were able to regenerate themselves after the e-commerce influx, focused upon establishing new structures that included the following features:

- **A user-friendly and secure e-commerce platform;**
- **A reconfiguration of their supply-chain to accommodate online orders;**
- **Implementation of an integrated technology infrastructure to support online and offline operations;**
- **New recruitment and employee training approaches.**

The overall purpose of the retail organization may not have changed. Nonetheless its underlying structure experienced an "ecological succession." New "species" that were not previously present in the brick-and-mortar era – like digital market analysts – were now part of the ecosystem. The process of regeneration contributed to a reconfiguration of the retail organization.

Regeneration of a business to a new state is only possible if an organization's networks are flexible and able to reconfigure themselves in the face of a disruption.

---

[72] www.britannica.com/science/ecological-succession

An organization that failed to make the e-commerce transition is the company Toys "R" Us (Basiouny, 2018). They initially underestimated the significance of e-commerce in its retail landscape. As a result, Toys "R" Us did not create the internal structures that were necessary to support their own autonomous online sales channel.

In the year 2000, Toys "R" Us agreed to a 10-year partnership with Amazon. As part of this agreement, it agreed to pay $50 million a year plus an additional percentage on all sales completed to Amazon in order to secure the online retailer as the exclusive online channel for its toys and baby products.

Toys "R" Us did not develop any of their own in-house systems. Instead, their online purchasers were immediately redirected to Amazon's website. Initially, the partnership worked well. Eventually, Amazon grasped how the Toys "R" Us business functioned. It began to sell toys and baby products from Toys "R" Us competitors. Even though Toys "R" Us sued Amazon and won, it was too late. Toys "R" Us had squandered years. During this time, it could have established its own internal online sales channel structures. In the meantime, Amazon had become Toys "R" Us biggest competitor. Toys "R" Us filed for bankruptcy In September of 2017 (Basiouny, 2018).

To ensure a healthy regenerative response to disturbances, leadership's role is to support the flexibility of its network structures which allow the network to reconfigure itself as circumstances require.

Symbiosis

The concepts of regeneration and evolution are interrelated. Regeneration enables individual organisms to recover from injuries or environmental stress. Evolution occurs over multiple generations. It involves changes in the genetic makeup of populations, ultimately leading to adaptations that improve survival and reproduction.

Both processes are governed by natural selection. In regenerative processes, the gene pool does not change even if the composition of species in the ecosystem changes. Evolution on the other hand, gives rise to an actual change in species. This change allows species to better adapt to their environment.

After the introduction of Darwin's seminal work on the **Origin of Species** in the 19th century, the key driver of evolution was believed to be competition (Spencer, 1884). This understanding persists even into the present day. It asserts that evolution occurs via chance mutations in the gene pool and natural selection. Only those species that can pass on their genes to the next generation have the capacity to influence the course of future evolution. Herbert Spencer famously coined the phrase "survival of the fittest" to capture this prevalent viewpoint (Spencer, 1884, p. 445).

A correction of this narrative has been provided by research in the fields of biology and ecology in the twenty-first century. Other processes for the evolution of the gene pool have been discovered such as gene flow, genetic drift,[73] and symbiosis. Symbiosis is the interaction between two or more different species that live together in a mutually beneficial relationship.[74] Symbiosis is currently considered one of the most powerful forces in evolution.

Co-operation not competition is the key driver of evolution.

What can leaders of organizations learn from this shift in perspective? Nature provides us with powerful examples.

Lichens are a composite organism that evolved from a symbiotic relationship between a fungus and a photosynthetic partner.[75] The fungus provides a protective environment and extracts nutrients from the surroundings. The green algae or cyanobacterium (or both) produces food through photosynthesis.

Lichens played a crucial role in the process of soil formation (see Figure 24) in the early years of this planet. This soil allowed plants to colonize the land from the sea. As organisms moved from aquatic environments to terrestrial ones, it was a considerable challenge for plants to inhabit the barren land. Lichens were among the pioneering organisms (Asta & Fournier, 2019) that could thrive in harsh, rocky environments. Lichens produce organic acids that

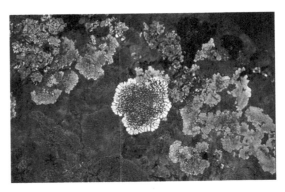

Figure 24 Lichens on a rock. Image from https://bouldercountyopenspace.org/i/science/why-like-lichens/

---

[73] https://bioprinciples.biosci.gatech.edu/module-1-evolution/neutral-mechanisms-of-evolution/
[74] https://en.wikipedia.org/wiki/Symbiosis
[75] This partner can be a green algae or a cyanobacterium or both.

break down minerals in rocks. This in turn leads to soil formation and the release of nutrients that are essential for plant growth.

Neither the fungus nor the algae could have created the conditions for soil formation and plant growth alone. Only the lichen that emerged from symbiosis had this capacity.

The Role of Leaders in Transformation

There is a lot of talk about transformation in today's V.U.C.A. world. The new title of Chief Transformation Officer is surging. Many consider an organization's transformation to be a process of evolution.

Actually, most organizations are struggling with regeneration, not evolution. The essence of an organization does not radically change when an e-commerce capability is integrated into its business. In other words, despite substantial changes, the DNA of the business does not necessarily change.

In the past years, many organizations have invested heavily to acquire a broad spectrum of digital capabilities. Despite these investments, most of these organizations still cling to the model of a "Machine Bureaucracy" and are still firmly invested in the paradigm that competition is the main driver of innovation.

Networks and network science are telling a different story. Most innovations arise from new connections.

The evolution of Assa Abloy[76] emerged by its ability to transform itself from a lock maker to an access provider. This transformation was enabled by reaching out and creating relationships with manufacturers of control systems and system integrators. As a result of cultivating these new connections, Assa Abloy was eventually able to enter completely different market niches.

The key to evolution in human social networks is
seeking and finding mutually beneficial symbiotic relationships.

The message that leaders need to cultivate symbiotic relationships to transform their organizations is unambiguous. Often those connections are to be found outside of their organizations. These novel connections have the potential to transform the very nature of an organization in the manner that the Assa Abloy transformation clearly illustrates.

A circular economy can only emerge through the formation of multiple symbiotic relationships which transcend the boundaries between organizations.

---

[76] For more details on the Assa Abloy story, see Part 4, pp. 57–58 from this Cambridge Leadership Elements.

Society & Planet

As illustrated by the example of the Great Barrier Reef, an ecosystem may not be able to return to a state of homeostasis when the environmental stress becomes too great.

This is a reminder for leaders to take a tough look at the health of their entire organization. It may look healthy. However, if it is surrounded by an unhealthy environment, the organization's capacity to adapt may be diminished.

"To thrive or not to thrive" that is the key question for network leaders. To thrive, leadership must promote the health of all dimensions of the system. This will require a fine-tuning to the special needs at each level: from individuals and teams to clusters, organizations, communities, and ultimately the needs of our planet. As both biology and network science have revealed, if any of the elements in this continuum are unhealthy, then the entire system will be unhealthy.

What is your company doing for the environment?
Ray Anderson, Former CEO, Interface®

A systemic problem requires a systemic response. Everyone is responsible for the health of our planet. The response is not a task to be abdicated to government nor an anticipated *deus-ex-machina* technological solution.

A systemic response to this global challenge by the company Interface®, started with a personal revelation by its former CEO Ray Anderson. Despite being a very successful company financially, he realized that its production practices were destroying the health of the planet. In his book "**Confessions of a Radical Industrialist**" (Anderson & Lanier, 2019), he recognized that the path to sustainability would be steep and challenging. Everyone in the organization needed to buy into this sustainability quest and actively cooperate to realize this common goal.

In 1997 "Mission Zero" was launched, a bid to reach net zero emissions by 2020. The culture started to transform itself as it began to collectively embrace the ambition of companywide sustainability. Employees began to see the changes that their recommendations were inspiring. Their active participation was key to awakening the innovative spirit throughout the organization. Interface® became a certified Carbon Neutral enterprise across its entire global business, products, and value chain in 2019. The future-driven business paradigm for success "*Doing well by doing good*" has motivated Interface® employees to build a very successful and environmentally friendly company during its 50-year history (Melhus, 2008). Their next goal is to focus on circularity and by so doing become a carbon negative enterprise by 2040 – a project that has been dubbed "Climate Take Back" (Makower, 2016).

As Ray Anderson recognized in his own company, the prevailing economic paradigm of today is untenable – unlimited growth is not possible on a finite planet. Encouraging health at all levels of the system points to the need to re-think how the current economic system should be transformed.

The Well-Being Economic Alliance was formed in 2018.[77] This alliance is a global cooperation of organizations, movements, and individuals who are working to transform the current economic system into a well-being circular economy. A well-being economy is based on meeting both human and planetary needs in a sustainable and equitable way. It is not based on economic growth as an end in and of itself (Capra & Jakobsen, 2017).

One of the initiatives of the Alliance is the Well-Being Economy Governments Partnership (WEGo). This initiative provides a forum to share expertise and transferrable policy practices among national governments. Currently the governments of New Zealand, Scotland, Wales, Finland, Iceland, and Canada are members. These members strive to deepen their understanding, co-create, and test alternative well-being focused visions of economic development while learning from each other's experiences and best practices.

The WEGo members offer an exemplary network response to a complex network issue.

Final Remarks

Networks challenge us to perceive organizations not as mere machines, but as living ecosystems. Similar to coral reefs, organizations exhibit intricate and interwoven structures that foster dynamic interactions among their elements. The role of network leadership is to nurture a vibrant ecosystem throughout an organization and its external partners. From this perspective, an organization is a living system, in which its diverse components coalesce harmoniously. This capacity enables all parts of an organization to adapt to change and by so doing, collectively enhance growth and resilience.

This Cambridge Elements is dedicated to exploring the nascent concept of Network Leadership. Fritjof Capra, physicist, systems theorist, and deep ecologist, has inspired much of the thinking of this publication. Capra's work is characterized by a unique interdisciplinary approach to science that combines insights from physics, biology, and systems theory. Out of his attentive reflections of the emerging science in each of these areas, a new understanding of reality based on the interconnectedness of all living systems has emerged.

---

[77] https://weall.org/about-weall

During a recent presentation to alumni of his Capra Course[78], he proposed a condensed synopsis of his view of life into four fundamental principles (Gamble, 2021). These principles are applicable for all living organisms from bacteria to human beings, and by extrapolation, to organizations and communities as well.

These four principles provide network leaders with insightful guidance when faced with the inevitable challenges of leadership.

> Life organizes itself in networks
> Life is inherently regenerative
> Life is inherently creative
> Life is inherently intelligent

These principles infer that the role of leadership is to provide the conditions for networks to identify solutions. It is not about solving problems. By trusting life's creativity and intelligence coupled with its regenerative capabilities, leaders will gain the capacity to resolve the most intractable problems not only in their organizations and ecosystems but on our planet as well.

Nature shows us that even under the most hostile conditions, life finds a way. The nuclear meltdown at Chernobyl in 1986 led to the immediate destruction of vegetation in the vicinity of the nuclear reactor. Animals that lived in the vicinity either died or migrated away from the region. One species however has thrived – cryptococcus neoformans[79], a type of fungus. Research suggests that this type of fungus is attracted to radiation. It can convert ionizing radiation into a form of energy. This provides the means for the environment around Chernobyl to eventually regenerate itself.

What is the lesson for leaders?

First and foremost, leaders need to focus on the **health** of the broad spectrum of networks that they serve – whether it be the health of individuals, teams, clusters, or outside stakeholders such as communities, business ecosystems, and the environment.

Secondly, they need to put an appropriate framework for positive action such as a compelling purpose and an enabling network structure in place.

And finally, leaders need to develop a deep-seated trust that the regenerative, creative, and intelligent capabilities of networks will take care of the rest.

---

[78] www.capracourse.net/ [79] https://en.wikipedia.org/wiki/Radiotrophic_fungus

References

Adner, R. (2021). *Winning the Right Game: How to Disrupt, Defend, and Deliver in a Changing World*. The MIT Press. 9780262045469.

Agile Marketing Case Studies (2018, June 1). *Case Study: Coca-Cola*. study.com. https://study.com/academy/lesson/agile-marketing-case-studies.html.

Al Galidi, R. (2021). *The Three Princes of Serendip: New Tellings of Old Tales for Everyone*. Candlewick. 978-1536214505.

Alexander, M.E.; Kobes, R. (2011). *Effects of vaccination and population structure on influenza epidemic spread in the presence of two circulating strains*. BMC Public Health. 11 (Suppl 1), S8. https://doi.org/10.1186/1471-2458-11-S1-S8.

Anderson, R.; Lanier, J. (2019). *Mid-Course Correction Revisited: The Story and Legacy of a Radical Industrialist and His Quest for Authentic Change*. Chelsea Green. 978-1-60358-889-8.

Anderson, R.; White, R. (2009). *Confessions of a Radical Industrialist: How Interface Proved You Can Build a Successful Business without Destroying the Planet*. St. Martins Press. 978-0312543495.

Arena, M.J. (2018). *Adaptive Space: How GM and Other Companies Are Positively Disrupting Themselves and Transforming into Agile Organizations*. McGraw Hill. 978-1-26-011803-2.

Arena, M.J. (2023). *Leveraging Social Capital: Effective Strategies for Intentional Collaboration in the New World of Work*. HR Exchange. www.hrexchangenetwork.com/employee-engagement/columns/effective-strategies-for-intentional-collaboration-in-the-new-world-of-work.

Arena, M.J. (2023, June 22). *Connections Matter More than Ever*. Biola University. Webinar.

Ashcroft, P.; Brown, S.; Garrick, J. (2020). *The Curious Advantage*. Laiki. 978-1-648871-369-9.

Asta, J.; Fournier, J. (2019). *Lichens, Surprising Pioneering Organisms*. Encyclopedia of the Environment. www.encyclopedie-environnement.org/en/life/lichens-pioneering-organisms/#:~:text=Lichens%20grow%20very%20slowly%20and,date%20back%20to%20the%20Devonian.

Bahrami, H. (1992). The emerging flexible organization: Perspective from Silicon Valley. *California Management Review*. 34(4), 33–52. https://doi.org/10.2307/41166702.

Barabási, A. L.; Frangos, J. (2002). *Linked: How Everything Is Connected to Everything Else and What It Means for Business, Science and Everday Life.* Perseus. 978-0-465-03861-9.

Barabási, A. L.; Pósfai, M. (2016). *Network Science.* Cambridge University Press. 978-1107076266.

Bartholomay, T.; Chazdon, S.; Marczak, M.; Walker, K. (2011). Mapping extension's networks: Using social network analysis to explore extension's outreach. *Journal of Extension.* 49, 29–42. https://doi.org/10.34068/joe.49.06.10.

Bartscherer, K. (2014, June 3). *Flatworms, the Masters of Regeneration – but Nothing Happens without Stem Cells.* Max Planck Institute for Molecular Biomedicine. www.mpg.de/8244494/flatworms-regeneration.

Basiouny, A. (2018, March 14). *What Went Wrong: The Demise of Toys R US.* Knowledge at Wharton Podcast. https://knowledge.wharton.upenn.edu/podcast/knowledge-at-wharton-podcast/the-demise-of-toys-r-us/.

Beeson, J. C. (2021, December 1). *Leadership Development which Integrates Learning with Teaching.* EnsembleEnabler.com. www.ensembleenabler.com/blog-en/agile-leadership-development/.

Beeson, J. C. (2023, July 30). *Shifting from a V.U.C.A. to a W.I.S.E. World.* LinkedIn. www.linkedin.com/pulse/shifting-from-vuca-wise-world-jeffrey-beeson-mba-ma/?trackingId=%2FL9vOG3qTWOhyTSXXOpOMg%3D%3D.

Belardinelli, G. (2019). *Gatekeepers in Social Networks: Logics for Communicative Actions.* Univesiteit van Amsterdam. MSc Thesis.

Belbin, R. M. (1981). *Management Teams: Why They Succeed or Fail.* Elsevier Science & Technology Books. 9780434901272.

Bennis, W. G. (1989). *On Becoming a Leader.* Addison-Wesley. 978-0783208176.

Bennis, W. G.; Nanus, B. (1985). *Leaders: Strategies for Taking Charge.* HarperCollins. 978-0887308390.

Bernier, K. (2022). *Beware of Gatekeepers.* https://medium.com/zentangle-art-and-more/beware-of-gatekeepers-93dfcef6e26a.

Bishop, T. (2015, June 25). *Exclusive: Satya Nadella Reveals Microsoft's New Mission Statement, Sees "Tough Choices" Ahead.* GeekWire. www.geekwire.com/2015/exclusive-satya-nadella-reveals-microsofts-new-mission-statement-sees-more-tough-choices-ahead/#:~:text=Every%20great%20company%20has%20an,our%20customers%20deeply%20care%20about.

Blackledge, S. (2023, February 3). *What Happens when the Pacific Loses Its Otters?* Environment America. https://environmentamerica.org/articles/what-happens-when-the-pacific-loses-its-otters/.

Britannica, T. Editors of Encyclopaedia (2023, November 10). *Resonance.* Encyclopedia Britannica. www.britannica.com/science/resonance-vibration.

Brittain, S. (2019). *The Ins & Outs of Organisational Network Analysis.* https://clearvoicecomms.co.uk/what-is-organisational-network-analysis-ona/.

Buchanan, M. (2002). *Nexus – Small Worlds and the Groundbreaking Science of Networks.* W.W. Norton. 978-0-393-07608-0.

Burns, J. M. (1978). *Leadership.* Harper & Row. 0060105887.

Busch, C. (2022). *Connect the Dots – The Art and Science of Creating Good Luck.* Penguin Life.

Buterin, V. (2014). *Ethereum: A Next Generation Smart Contract and Decentralized Application Platform.* ethereum.org. https://ethereum.org/en/whitepaper/.

Capra, F.; Jakobsen, O. D. (2017, June 12). A conceptual framework for ecological economics based on systemic principles of life. *International Journal of Social Economics.* 44(6), 831–844. https://doi.org/10.1108/IJSE-05-2016-0136.

Capra, F.; Luisi, P. L. (2014). *The Systems View of Life.* Cambridge University Press. 978-1-107-01136-6.

Carlson, S. C. (2023, July 7). *Königsberg Bridge Problem.* Encyclopedia Britannica. www.britannica.com/science/Konigsberg-bridge-problem.

Chan, S. (2001). *Complex Adaptive Systems.* Massachussetts Institute of Technology. https://web.mit.edu/esd.83/www/notebook/Complex%20Adaptive%20Systems.pdf.

Christakis, N.; Fowler, J. (2009). *Connected: The Amazing Power of Social Networks and How They Shape Our Lives.* HarperCollins. 978-0007303601.

Cohen, R. (2022, July 14). *France Faces a Shortage of Mustard, Its Uniquely Beloved Condiment.* New York Times. www.nytimes.com/2022/07/14/world/europe/france-mustard-shortage-dijon.html.

Collins, J. C. (2002). *Built to Last* (3rd ed.). HarperBusiness. 978-0060516406.

Conti, R. (2022, August 27). *Understanding EOS and EOSIO.* Forbes Advisor. www.forbes.com/advisor/investing/cryptocurrency/eos-eosio/.

Covey, S. R. (1990). *The 7 Basic Habits of Highly Effective People: Restoring the character Ethic.* 1st Fireside ed. Fireside Book.

Cross, R. (2021). *Beyond Collaboration Overload: How to Work Smarter, Get Ahead, and Restore Your Well-Being.* Harvard Business Review Press. 978-1647820121.

Cross, R. (Accessed September 8, 2023). *Drive Organizational Change through Network Influencers.* rob.cross.org. www.robcross.org/drive-organizational-change-through-network-influencers/.

Cross, R. (Accessed September 8, 2023). *What Is Organizational Network Analysis?* robcross.org. www.robcross.org/what-is-organizational-network-analysis/.

Cross, R.; Baker, W.; Parker, A. (2003, July 15). *What Creates Energy in Organizations?* MIT Sloan Management Review. Magazine Summer / Research Feature. https://sloanreview.mit.edu/article/what-creates-energy-in-organizations/.

Dahl, C. J.; Wilson-Mendenhall, C. D.; Davidson, R. J. (2020). *The Plasticity of Well-Being: A Training-Based Framework for the Cultivation of Human Flourishing.* Center for Healthy Minds. https://centerhealthyminds.org/assets/files-publications/Dahl-The-plasticity-of-well-being.pdf.

Davidson, R. (2022, September 1). *Well-Being Is a Skill.* Mind & Life Institute. www.mindandlife.org/insight/well-being-is-a-skill/.

Dietzel, A.; Bode, M.; Connolly, S. (2020, October 14). *Long-Term Shifts in the Colony Size Structure of Coral Populations along the Great Barrier Reef.* The Royal Society. https://doi.org/10.1098/rspb.2020.1432.

Diller, T. (2021). *Buurtzorg – Leuchtturm für Selbstorganisation.* thomasdiller.com. www.thomasdiller.com/2021/09/10/buurtzorg/.

Drucker, P. (1974). *Management: Tasks, Responsibilities, Practices.* Harper & Row. 0434903981.

Dunbar, R. I. M. (1992). Neocortex size as a constraint on group size in primates. *Journal of Human Evolution.* 22(6), 469–493. https://doi.org/10.1016/0047-2484(92)90081-J.

Edmondson, A. C. (2018). *The Fearless Organization: Creating Psychological Safety in the Workplace for Learning, Innovation, and Growth.* John Wiley & Sons. 9781119477242.

Ehrlichmann, D. (2021). *Impact Networks: Create Connection, Spark Collaboration and Catalyze Systemic Change.* Berrett-Koehler. 978-1-5230-9168-3.

Estrada, E. (2011). *The Structure of Complex Networks: Theory and Applications.* Oxford University Press.978-0199591756

Euler, L. (1741). *Solutio problematis ad geometriam situs pertinentis*, Eneström 53, MAA Euler Archive.

Farahani, F.; Karwowski, W.; Lighthall, N. (2019). *Application of Graph Theory for Identifying Connectivity Patterns in Human Brain Networks: A Systematic Review.* Frontiers in Neuroscience. 13. 585. https://doi.org/10.3389/fnins.2019.00585.

Ferguson, N. (2018). *The Square and the Tower: Networks, Hierarchies and the Struggle for Global Power.* Penguin Books. 978-0-141-98482-7.

Fiedler, F. (1964). A Contigency Model of Leadership Effectiveness. *Advances in Experimental Social Psychology.* 1, 149–190.

Fischer, B. (2021, November 5). *No Managers, More Leaders: The Leadership Legacy of Zhang Ruimin.* Forbes. www.forbes.com/sites/billfischer/2021/11/05/no-managers-more-leaders-the-leadership-legacy-of-zhang-ruimin/?sh=16b5dc72908c.

Fisk, P. (2015, November 6). *Haier's "Rendanheyi" Business Model.* peterfisk.com. www.peterfisk.com/2015/11/haier-thinking/.

Foster, R.; Kaplan, S. (2001). *Creative Destruction: Why Companies that Are Built to Last Underperform the Market – and How to Successfully Transform Them.* Financial Times Prentice Hall. https://hbswk.hbs.edu/archive/creative-destruction-why-companies-that-are-built-to-last-underperform-the-market-and-how-to-successfully-transform-them.

Fridovich-Keil, J. L.; Rogers, K. (2023, November 7). *Epigenetics.* Encyclopedia Britannica. www.britannica.com/science/epigenetics.

Gamble, M. (2021, November 26). *What Is Life? Fritjof Capra Explains the 4 Characteristics of Life – Video.* Permaculture Education Institute. www.youtube.com/watch?v=Moe_4iC6kBg.

Gertner, J. (2023, July 18). *Wikipedia's Moment of Truth.* New York Times. www.nytimes.com/2023/07/18/magazine/wikipedia-ai-chatgpt.html, accessed August 16, 2023.

Granovetter, M. (1973). The strength of weak ties. *American Journal of Sociology.* 78, 1360–1380. https://doi.org/10.1086/225469.

Greenleaf, R. K. (1996). *On Becoming a Servant Leader: The Private Writings of Robert K. Greenleaf.* Jossey-Bass. 978-0470422007.

Guare, J. (1990). *Six Degrees of Separation: A Play* (1st ed.). Random House. 978-0413672308.

Gulick, M. K. (accessed September 12, 2023). *Our Moral Endowment: The Human Journey.* https://humanjourney.us/intercultural/our-moral-endowment/.

Hackman, J. R.; Vidmar, N. (1970). Effects of size and task type on group performance and member reactions. *Sociometry.* 33(1), 37–54

Hagel III, J. (2021). *The Journey Beyond Fear: Leverage the Three Pillars of Positivity to Build Your Success.* McGraw Hill. 978-1264268405.

Hagel III, J.; Seely Brown, J.; Davison, L. (2010). *The Power of Pull: How Small Moves, Smartly Made, Can Set Big Things in Motion.* Basic Books. 978-0-465-02113-0.

Hamel, G.; Zanini, M. (2020). *Humanocracy, Creating Organizations as Amazing as the People Inside Them.* Harvard Business Review Press. 978-1633696020.

Handy, C. B. (1994). *The Age of Paradox*. Harvard Business Press. 978-0875846439.

Kagan, J. (2019, January 7). *How Microsoft Lost the Wireless Smartphone Wars*. Computerworld. www.computerworld.com/article/3331139/how-microsoft-lost-the-wireless-smartphone-wars.html.

Kaptchuk, T. J. (2000). *The Web that Has No Weaver: Understanding Chinese Medicine*. Contemporary Books. 978-0809228409.

Kashdan, T. (2009). *Curious? Discover the Missing Ingredient to a Fulfilling Life*. William Morrow. 978-0061661198.

Keltner, D. (2023). *Awe – The Transformative Power of Everyday Wonder*. Penguin Books. 9780241624104.

Kouzes, J. M.; Posner, B. Z. (2022). *The Leadership Challenge: How to Make Extraordinary Things Happen in Organizations*. Josey-Bass. 978-1119736127.

Kronauer, D. (2022, July 20). *Ant Colonies Behave Like Neural Networks when Making Decisions*. The Rockefeller University. www.rockefeller.edu/news/32489-ant-colonies-behave-like-neural-networks-when-making-decisions.

Kuchler, H.; Abboud, L. (2021, February 16). *Why the Three Biggest Vaccine Makers Failed on Covid 19*. Financial Times. https://www.ft.com/content/657b123a-78ba-4fba-b18e-23c07e313331.

Kuhn, T. S. (1962). *The Structure of Scientific Revolutions*. University of Chicago Press. 0-226-45808-3.

Laloux, F. (2014). *Reinventing Organizations: A Guide to Creating Organizations Inspired by the Next Stage in Human Consciousness*. Nelson Parker. 978-2960133516.

Lent, J. (2017). *The Patterning Instinct: A Cultural History of Humanity's Search for Meaning*. Prometheus. 978-1633882935.

Lent, J. (2021). *The Web of Meaning: Integrating Science and Traditional Wisdom to Find Our Place in the Universe*. Profile. 978-1788165655.

Levy, M.; Stewart, D. E.; Kent, C. H. W. (accessed August 14, 2023). *Encyclopædia Britannica*. Encyclopedia Britannica. www.britannica.com/topic/Encyclopaedia-Britannica-English-language-reference-work.

Loewenstein, G. (1994). *The Psychology of Curiosity: A Review and Reinterpretation*. Psychological Bulletin. 116(1), 75–98. https://doi.org/10.1037/0033-2909.116.1.75.

Lu, Z.; Wahlström, J.; Nehorai, A. (2018, April). Community detection in complex networks via clique conductance. *Scientific Reports*. 8(5982), 1–16.

Lutkevich, B. (accessed Sep 6, 2023). *What Is the Waterfall Model?* Tech Target Network. www.techtarget.com/searchsoftwarequality/definition/waterfall-model.

MacDonald, J. (2018). *When Crown-of-Thorns Starfish Attack.* JSTOR. https://daily.jstor.org/when-crown-of-thorns-starfish-attack/.

Magnuson, W. (2020). *Blockchain Democracy: Technology, Law and the Rule of the Crowd.* Cambridge University Press. 978-1-108-48236-3.

Maienschein, J.; MacCord, K. (2022). *What Is Regeneration?* University of Chicago Press. 978-0226816562.

Makower, J. (2016, June 6). *Inside Interface's Bold New Mission to Achieve "Climate Take Back."* GreenBiz. www.greenbiz.com/article/inside-inter faces-bold-new-mission-achieve-climate-take-back.

McCarthy, J. D.; Zald, N. M. (1977). Resource Mobilization and Social Movements: A Partial Theory. *American Journal of Sociology.* 82(6), 1212–1241.

Melhus, P. J. (2008). *Doing Well by Doing Good.* VDM Verlag Dr. Mueller e.K. 9783639085785.

Milgram, S. (1967). The Small World Problem. *Psychology Today.* 2, 60–67.

Millegan, C.; Berry, P.; Burnett, J.; Williams, R. (2018). *Blockbuster Failure! Ignoring Innovation Is Not a Strategy.* academia.edu. https://www.academia.edu/36564159/Blockbuster_Failure_Ignoring_Innovation_is_Not_a_Strategy.

Minaar, J. (2022, September 14). *The EMC Contract as a Smart Coordination Mechanism.* Global Focus Magazine. www.globalfocusmagazine.com/the-emc-contract-as-a-smart-coordination-mechanism/.

Minaev, A. (2023, June 28). *A Complete History of DAOs (1960s-NOW).* Cryptodose.net. https://cryptodose.net/learn/history-of-daos/.

Mintzberg, H. (1980). Structure in 5's: A synthesis of the research on organization design. *Management Science.* 26(3), 322–341. https://doi.org/10.1287/mnsc.26.3.322.

Osman, A. (2023). *What Is the Network Effect?* WSO Academy. www.wall streetoasis.com/resources/skills/economics/what-is-network-effect.

Paine, R. T. (1969). A note on trophic complexity and community stability. *American Naturalists.* 103, 91–93.

Palus, S.; Bródka, P.; Kazienko, P. (2010, September). How to analyze company using social network. *DBLP: Communications in Computer and Information Science.* 111, 159–164. https://doi.org10.1007/978-16318-0_18.

Paradise, C. J.; Campbell, A. M. (2016). *Ecological Homeostasis.* Momentum Press. 9781606509562.

Pisani, F. (2007). Interview with Fritjof Capra. *International Journal of Communication.* 1(1), 21. https://ijoc.org/index.php/ijoc/article/view/69.

Podolny, J. M.; Hansen, M. T. (2020, November–December). *How Apple Is Organized for Innovation.* Harvard Business Review.

Pollack, J.; Pollack, R. (2015). *Using Kotter's Eight Stage Process to Manage an Organisational Change Program: Presentation and Practice*. Systemic Practice and Action Research. https://doi.org/10.1007/s11213-014-9317-0.

Popper, K. (1945). *The Open Society and Its Enemies*. Routledge. 978-0415610216.

Ptahhotep (2016). *The Teachings of Ptahhotep: The Oldest Book in the World*. Watchmaker. 978-1603867399.

Putnam, R. D. (2000). *Bowling Alone: Revised and Updated: The Collapse and Revival of American Community*. Simon & Schuster. 978-0684832838.

Quintarelli, E. (2021, August 23). *How Rendanheyi Helped Fujitsu Gain Agility towards Customer Demand*. Stories of Platform Design. https://stories.platformdesigntoolkit.com/how-rendanheyi-helped-fujitsu-gain-agility-towards-customer-demand-bfeacedcb450.

Quintarelli, E. (2021, December 31). *Going Beyond Agile through the Rendanheyi at Bosch: Stories of Platform Design*. https://stories.platformdesigntoolkit.com/going-beyond-agile-through-the-rendanheyi-at-bosch-917b69ce966a.

Raymond, E. S. (2001). *The Cathedral & the Bazaar: Musings on Linux and Open Source by an Accidental Revolutionary*. O'Reilly and Associates. 978-0596001087.

Reichheld, F. (2011). *The Ultimate Question 2.0: How Net Promoter Companies Thrive in a Customer-Driven World*. Harvard Business Press. 978-1422173350.

Richter, F. (2020, January 11). *How Did Microsoft Fare in the Post-Bill Gates Era?* statista. www.statista.com/chart/20469/microsofts-share-price-since-bill-gates-stepped-down-as-ceo/.

Ridley, M. (2016, January 6). *What Is the Perfect Team Size?* LinkedIn. www.linkedin.com/pulse/whats-perfect-team-size-mark-ridley.

Robertson, B. J. (2015). *Holocracy: The New Management System for a Rapidly Changing World*. Henry Holt. 978-1627794282.

Rugnetta, M. (2023, December 14). *Neuroplasticity*. Encyclopedia Britannica. www.britannica.com/science/neuroplasticity.

Scharmer, C. O. (2016). *Theory U*. Berrett-Koehler. 978-1626567986.

Schein, E. H. (1989). *Organizational Culture and Leadership*. Jossey-Bass Management Series. 9781119212041.

Schein, E. H. (2013).*Humble Inquiry: The Gentle Art of Asking Instead of Telling*. Berrett-Koehler. 978-1-60994-981-5.

Schein, E. H.; Schein, P. A. (2018). *Humble Leadership: The Power of Relationships, Openness, and Trust*. Berrett-Koehler. 978-1-5230-9538-4.

Schlechty, P. C. (2004). *Shaking Up the Schoolhouse: How to Support and Sustain Educational Innovation*. Wiley. 978-0787972134.

Scollon, C. N.; Kim-Prieto,C.; Diener, E. (2003). Experience Sampling: Promise and Pitfalls, Strengths and Weaknesses. *Journal of Happiness Studies*. 4, 5–34.

Senge, P. M. (1990). *The Fifth Discipline: The Art and Practice of the Learning Organization*. Doubleday. 978-0385260954.

Senge, P. M.; Scharmer, C. O.; Jaworski, J.; Flowers, B. S. (2004). *Presence: Human Purpose and the Field of the Future*. Crown Business. 978-0385516303.

Shah, H. (2019). *The Most Important Turning Points in Microsoft's History*. Nira Blog. https://nira.com/microsoft-history/.

Shapera, M. N.; Krstic, M. N. (2008). *ONA Analysis: The Unbeatable Power of Organizational Networks*. HR World Magazine. no. 8. https://hrworld.org/ona-analysis-the-unbeatable-power-of-organizational-networks/.

Sharma, R. (2023). *5 Types of Binary Tree Explained with Illustrations*. upGrad.com. www.upgrad.com/blog/5-types-of-binary-tree/.

Simard, S. (2021). *Finding the Mother Tree: Discovering the Wisdom of the Forest*. Random House. 978-0593459423.

Sinek, S. (2011). *Start with Why: How Great Leaders Inspire Everyone to Take Action*. Penguin Books. 978-1591846444.

Smith, A. (1776). *The Wealth of Nations Vol. IV*. The University of Chicago Press. 978-0226763743.

Sozen H. C.; Sagsan, M. (2010). The Brokerage Roles in the Organizational Network and Manipulation of Information Flow. *International Journal of eBusiness and eGovernment Studies*. 2(2), 41–51.

Spencer, H. (1884). *The Principles of Biology, Vol. 1*. Cornell University Library. 978-1112057540.

Stadler, C.; Hautz, J.; Matzler, K.; Von den Eichen, S. F. (2021). *Open Strategy: Mastering Disruption Outside the C-Suite*. The MIT Press. 978-0262046114.

Steiber, A. (2022). *Leadership for a Digital World: The Transformation of GE Appliances*. Springer. 978-3030957537.

Steiber, A.; Alänge, S. (2015). *The Silicon Valley Model – Management for Entrepreneurship*. Springer. 978-3319249193.

Sun, X.; Wandelt, S. (2021). Robustness of Air Transportation as Complex Networks: Systematic Review of 15 Years of Research and Outlook into the Future. *Sustainability*. 13(11), 6446. https://doi.org/10.3390/su13116446.

Talas, A. (2021, September 9). *Connected: How Kevin Bacon Cured Cancer – Video*. Curiosity Stream. https://curiositystream.com/video/4609.

Team Nuggets (2018, August 10). *Why Linux Runs 90 Percent of the Public Cloud Workload*. CBTnuggets. www.cbtnuggets.com/blog/certifications/open-source/why-linux-runs-90-percent-of-the-public-cloud-workload.

The Economist (2020, October 24). *How Satya Nadella Turned Microsoft Around*. economist.com. www.economist.com/briefing/2020/10/22/how-satya-nadella-turned-microsoft-around.

The Red Hat Enterprise Linux Team (2012, March 23). *Red Hat Enterprise Linux Powers the Globe's Stock Exchanges*. Red Hat. www.redhat.com/en/blog/red-hat-enterprise-linux-powers-the-globes-stock-exchanges.

Thomke, S. H. (2020). *Experimentation Works: The Surprising Power of Business Experiments*. Harvard Business Review Press. 978-16336 97102.

Tozzi, C. (2016, April 25). *Open Source and Android: A History of Google's Linux-Based Mobile OS*. Channel Futures. www.channelfutures.com/connectivity/open-source-and-android-a-history-of-google-s-linux-based-mobile-os.

Tuckman, B. (1965). *Developmental Sequence in Small Groups*. Psychological Bulletin. https://doi.org/10.1037/h0022100. PMID 14314073.

Vaughn-Nichols, S. (2017, November 14). *Linux Totally Dominates Supercomputers*. ZD Net. www.zdnet.com/article/linux-totally-dominates-supercomputers/.

Viguerie, S. P.; Calder, N.; Hindo, B. (2021). *2021 Corporate Longevity Forecast*. Innosight. www.innosight.com/wp-content/uploads/2021/05/Innosight_2021-Corporate-Longevity-Forecast.pdf.

Vos, C. (2008). *Buurtzorg Nederland: A Fresh View on Home Care*. workplaceinnovation.org. www.workplaceinnovation.org/kennis/buurtzorg-nederland-a-fresh-view-on-home-care/.

Wagner, R.; Harter, J. (2007, September 13). *The Fifth Element of Great Managing*. Gallup Business Journal. https://news.gallup.com/businessjournal/28561/fifth-element-great-managing.aspx.

Watanabe, K. (2021). *Network Effects Total Guide*. LinkedIn. www.linkedin.com/pulse/network-effects-total-guide-kei-watanabe/.

Watts, D. J. (2002). *Six Degrees: The Science of a Connected Age*. W.W. Norton. 978-0-393-07612-7.

Watts, D. J.; Strogatz, S. H. (1998). Collective dynamics of "small-world" networks. *Nature*. 393, 440–442. https://doi.org/10.1038/30918.

Williams, O. E.; Lacasa, L.; Latora, V. (2019). Quantifying and predicting success in show business. *Nature Communication*. 10, 2256. https://doi.org/10.1038/s41467-019-10213-0.

Witman, J.; Roy, K. (2009). *Marine Macroecology.* The University of Chicago Press. 978-0-226-90411-5.

Yeter, I. (2021, August 24). *First Proof of "Six Degrees of Separation."* neo4j. https://neo4j.com/developer-blog/first-proof-of-six-degrees-of-separation/.

Stella Nkomo, *University of Pretoria*
Rajnandini Pillai, *California State University, San Marcos*
Micha Popper, *University of Haifa*
Terry Price, *University of Richmond*
Krish Raval, *University of Oxford*
Roni Reiter-Palmon, *University of Nebraska*
Birgit Schyns, *Durham University*
Gillian Secrett, *University of Cambridge*
Nicholas Warner, *Claremont McKenna College*

in partnership with
Møller Centre, Churchill College
www.mollercentre.co.uk

The Møller Institute (www.mollerinstitute.com), home of the James McGregor Burns Academy of Leadership, brings together business and academia for practical leadership development and executive education. As part of Churchill College in the University of Cambridge, the Institute's purpose is to inspire individuals to be the best they can be, to accelerate the performance of the organizations which they serve, and, through our work, to covenant profits to Churchill College to support the education of future leaders. In everything we do our focus is to create a positive impact for people, society, and the Environment.

International Leadership Association
www.ila-net.org

The International Leadership Association (www.ila-net.org) is the organization for connecting leadership scholars, practitioners, and educators in ways that serve to enhance their learning, their understanding, and their impact in the world. These exchanges are professionally enriching, serve to elevate the field of leadership, and advance our mission to advance leadership knowledge and practice for a better world.

About the Series

Cambridge Elements in Leadership is multi- and inter-disciplinary, and will have broad appeal for leadership courses in Schools of Business, Education, Engineering, Public Policy, and in the Social Sciences and Humanities. In addition to the scholarly audience, Elements appeals to professionals involved in leadership development and training.

The series is published in partnership with the International Leadership Association (ILA) and the Møller Institute, Churchill College in the University of Cambridge.

Cambridge Elements ☰

Leadership

Elements in the Series

Printed in the United States
by Baker & Taylor Publisher Services